NOTES ON THE SYNTHESIS OF FORM

NOTES ON THE SYNTHESIS

OF FORM / *Christopher Alexander*

Harvard University Press
Cambridge, Massachusetts, and London, England

TO MY DEAREST JAN

Library of Congress Catalog Card Number 64-13417

ISBN 0-674-62751-2 (paper)
Printed in the United States of America

PREFACE TO THE PAPERBACK EDITION

Today, almost ten years after I wrote this book, one idea stands out clearly for me as the most important in the book: *the idea of the diagrams.*

These diagrams, which, in my more recent work, I have been calling *patterns*, are the key to the process of creating form. In this book I presented the diagrams as the end results of a long process; I put the accent on the process, and gave the diagrams themselves only a few pages of discussion. But once the book was finished, and I began to explore the process which I had described, I found that the diagrams themselves had immense power, and that, in fact, most of the power of what I had written lay in the power of these diagrams.

The idea of a diagram, or pattern, is very simple. It is an abstract pattern of physical relationships which resolves a small system of interacting and conflicting forces, and is independent of all other forces, and of all other possible diagrams. The idea that it is possible to create such abstract relationships one at a time, and to create designs which are whole by fusing these relationships—this amazingly simple idea is, for me, the most important discovery of the book.

I have discovered, since, that these abstract diagrams not only allow you to create a single whole from them, by fusion, but also have other even more important powers. Because the diagrams are independent of one another, you can study them and improve them one at a time, so that their evolution can be gradual and cumulative. More important still, because they are abstract and independent, you can use them to create not just one design, but an infinite variety of designs, all of them free combinations of the same set of patterns.

As you can see, it is the independence of the diagrams which gives them these powers. At the time I wrote this book, I was very much concerned with the formal definition of "independence," and the idea of using a mathematical method to discover systems of forces and diagrams which are independent. *But once the book was written, I discovered that it is quite unnecessary to use such a complicated and formal way of getting at the independent diagrams.*

If you understand the need to create independent diagrams, which resolve, or solve, systems of interacting human forces, you will find that you can create, and develop, these diagrams piecemeal, one at a time, in the most natural way, out of your experience of buildings and design, simply by thinking about the forces which occur there and the conflicts between these forces.

I have written about this realization and its consequences, in other, more recent works. But I feel it is important to say it also here, to make you alive to it before you read the book, since so many readers have focused on the *method which leads to* the creation of the diagrams, not on the *diagrams themselves*, and have even made a cult of following this method.

Indeed, since the book was published, a whole academic field has grown up around the idea of "design methods"—and I have been hailed as one of the leading exponents of these so-called design methods. I am very sorry that this has happened, and want to state, publicly, that I reject the whole idea of design methods as a subject of study, since I think it is absurd to separate the study of designing from the practice of design. In fact, people who study design methods without also practicing design are almost always frustrated designers who have no sap in them, who have lost, or never had, the urge to shape things. Such a person will never be able to say anything sensible about "how" to shape things either.

Poincaré once said: "Sociologists discuss sociological methods; physicists discuss physics." I love this statement. Study of method by itself is always barren, and people who have treated this book as if it were a book about "design method" have almost always missed the point of the diagrams, and their great importance, because they have been obsessed with the details of the method I propose for getting at the diagrams.

No one will become a better designer by blindly following this method, or indeed by following any method blindly. On the other hand, if you try to understand the idea that you can create abstract patterns by studying the implication of limited systems of forces, and can create new forms by free combination of these patterns—and realize that this will only work if the patterns which you define deal with systems of forces whose internal interaction is very dense, and whose interaction with the other forces in the world is very weak—then, in the process of trying to create such diagrams or patterns for yourself, you will reach the central idea which this book is all about.

C.A.

Berkeley, California
February 1971

CONTENTS

"First, the taking in of scattered particulars under one Idea, so that everyone understands what is being talked about ... Second, the separation of the Idea into parts, by dividing it at the joints, as nature directs, not breaking any limb in half as a bad carver might."

Plato, *Phaedrus*, 265D

These notes are about the process of design; the process of inventing physical things which display new physical order, organization, form, in response to function.

Today functional problems are becoming less simple all the time. But designers rarely confess their inability to solve them. Instead, when a designer does not understand a problem clearly enough to find the order it really calls for, he falls back on some arbitrarily chosen formal order. The problem, because of its complexity, remains unsolved.

Consider a simple example of a design problem, the choice of the materials to be used in the mass production of any simple household object like a vacuum cleaner. Time and motion studies show that the fewer different kinds of materials there are, the more efficient factory assembly is — and therefore demand a certain simplicity in the variety of materials used. This need for simplicity conflicts with the fact that the form will function better if we choose the best material for each separate purpose separately. But then, on the other hand, functional diversity of materials makes for expensive and complicated joints between components, which is liable to make maintenance less easy. Further still, all three issues, simplicity, performance, and jointing, are at odds with our desire to minimize the cost of the materials. For if we choose the cheapest material for each separate task, we shall not necessarily have simplicity, nor optimum performance, nor materials which can be cleanly jointed. Writing a minus sign beside a line for conflict, and a plus beside a line for positive agreement, we see that even this simple problem has the five-way conflict pictured below.

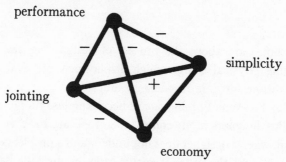

This is a typical design problem; it has requirements which have to be met; and there are interactions between the requirements, which makes the requirements hard to meet. This problem is simple to solve. It falls easily within the compass of a single man's intuition. But what about a more complicated problem?

Consider the task of designing a complete environment for a million people. The ecological balance of human and animal and plant life must be correctly adjusted both internally and to the given exterior physical conditions. People must be able to lead the individual lives they wish for. The social conditions induced must not lead to gross ill-health or to gross personal misery, and must not cause criminal delinquency. The cyclical intake of food and goods must not interfere with the regular movements of the inhabitants. The economic forces which

2

develop must not lead to real-estate speculation which destroys the functional relation between residential areas and areas supporting heavy goods. The transportation system must not be organized so that it creates a demand that aggravates its own congestion. People must somehow be able to live in close cooperation and yet pursue the most enormous variety of interests. The physical layout must be compatible with foreseeable future regional developments. The conflict between population growth and diminishing water resources, energy resources, parklands, must somehow be taken care of. The environment must be organized so that its own regeneration and reconstruction does not constantly disrupt its performance.

As in the simpler example, each of these issues interacts with several of the others. But in this case each issue is itself a vast problem; and the pattern of interactions is vastly complicated. The difference between these two cases is really like the difference between the problem of adding two and two, and the problem of calculating the seventh root of a fifty digit number. In the first case we can quite easily do it in our heads. In the second case, the complexity of the problem will defeat us unless we find a simple way of writing it down, which lets us break it into smaller problems.

Today more and more design problems are reaching insoluble levels of complexity. This is true not only of moon bases, factories, and radio receivers, whose complexity is internal, but even of villages and teakettles. In spite of their superficial simplicity, even these problems have a background of needs and activities which is becoming too complex to grasp intuitively.

To match the growing complexity of problems, there is a

3

growing body of information and specialist experience. This information is hard to handle; it is widespread, diffuse, unorganized.[1] Moreover, not only is the quantity of information itself by now beyond the reach of single designers, but the various specialists who retail it are narrow and unfamiliar with the form-makers' peculiar problems, so that it is never clear quite how the designer should best consult them.[2] As a result, although ideally a form should reflect all the known facts relevant to its design, in fact the average designer scans whatever information he happens on, consults a consultant now and then when faced by extra-special difficulties, and introduces this randomly selected information into forms otherwise dreamt up in the artist's studio of his mind. The technical difficulties of grasping all the information needed for the construction of such a form are out of hand — and well beyond the fingers of a single individual.[3]

At the same time that the problems increase in quantity, complexity, and difficulty, they also change faster than before. New materials are developed all the time, social patterns alter quickly, the culture itself is changing faster than it has ever changed before. In the past — even after the intellectual upheaval of the Renaissance — the individual designer would stand to *some* extent upon the shoulders of his predecessors. And although he was expected to make more and more of his own decisions as traditions gradually dissolved, there was always still some body of tradition which made his decisions easier. Now the last shreds of tradition are being torn from him. Since cultural pressures change so fast, any slow development of form becomes impossible. Bewildered, the form-maker stands alone. He has to make clearly conceived forms without the possibility of trial and error over time. He has

4

to be encouraged now to think his task through from the beginning, and to "create" the form he is concerned with, for what once took many generations of gradual development is now attempted by a single individual.[4] But the burden of a thousand years falls heavily on one man's shoulders, and this burden has not yet materially been lightened. The intuitive resolution of contemporary design problems simply lies beyond a single individual's integrative grasp.

Of course there are no definite limits to this grasp (especially in view of the rare cases where an exceptional talent breaks all bounds). But if we look at the lack of organization and lack of clarity of the forms around us, it is plain that their design has often taxed their designer's cognitive capacity well beyond the limit. The idea that the capacity of man's invention is limited is not so surprising, after all. In other areas it has been shown, and we admit readily enough, that there are bounds to man's cognitive and creative capacity. There are limits to the difficulty of a laboratory problem which he can solve;[5] to the number of issues he can consider simultaneously;[6] to the complexity of a decision he can handle wisely.[7] There are no absolute limits in any of these cases (or usually even any scale on which such limits could be specified); yet in practice it is clear that there are limits of some sort. Similarly, the very frequent failure of individual designers to produce well organized forms suggests strongly that there are limits to the individual designer's capacity.

We know that there are similar limits to an individual's capacity for mental arithmetic. To solve a sticky arithmetical problem, we need a way of setting out the problem which makes it perspicuous. Ordinary arithmetic convention gives us such a way. Two minutes with a pencil on the back of an envelope lets us solve problems which we could not do in our heads if we tried for a hundred years. But at present we have no corresponding way of simplifying design problems for ourselves. These notes describe a way of representing design problems which does make them easier to solve. It is a way of reducing the gap between the designer's small capacity and the great size of his task.

Part One contains a general account of the nature of design problems. It describes the way such problems have been solved in the past: first, in cultures where new problems are so rare that there are no actual designers; and then, by contrast, in cultures where new problems occur all the time, so that they have to be solved consciously by designers. From the contrast between the two, we shall learn how to represent a design problem so that it can be solved. Part Two describes the representation itself, and the kind of analysis the representation allows. Appendix 1 shows by example how the method works in practice.

The analysis of design problems is by no means obviously possible. There is a good deal of superstition among designers as to the deathly effect of analysis on their intuitions — with the unfortunate result that very few designers have tried to understand the process of design analytically. So that we get off to a fair start, let us try first to lay the ghosts which beset designers and make them believe that analysis is somehow at odds with the real problem of design.

It is not hard to see why the introduction of mathematics into design is likely to make designers nervous. Mathematics, in the popular view, deals with magnitude. Designers recognize, correctly, that calculations of magnitude only have strictly limited usefulness in the invention of form, and are therefore naturally rather skeptical about the possibility of basing design on mathematical methods.[8] What they do not realize, however, is that modern mathematics deals at least as much with questions of order and relation as with questions of magnitude. And though even this kind of mathematics may be a poor tool if used to prescribe the physical nature of forms, it can become a very powerful tool indeed if it is used to explore the conceptual order and pattern which a problem presents to its designer.

Logic, like mathematics, is regarded by many designers with suspicion. Much of it is based on various superstitions about the kind of force logic has in telling us what to do. First of all, the word "logic" has some currency among designers as a reference to a particularly unpleasing and functionally unprofitable kind of formalism.[9] The so-called logic of Jacques François Blondel or Vignola, for instance, referred to rules according to which the elements of architectural style could be combined.[10] As rules they may be logical. But this gives them no special force unless there is also a legitimate relation between the system of logic and the needs and forces we accept in the real world. Again, the cold visual "logic" of the steel-skeleton office building seems horribly constrained, and if we take it seriously as an intimation of what logic is likely to do, it is certain to frighten us away from analytical methods.[11] But no one shape can any more be a consequence of the use of logic than any other, and it is nonsense to blame rigid physical form on the rigidity of logic. It is not possible to set up premises, trace through a series of deductions, and arrive at a form which is logically determined by the premises, unless the premises already have the seeds of a particular

7

plastic emphasis built into them. There is no legitimate sense in which deductive logic can prescribe physical form for us.

But, in speaking of logic, we do not need to be concerned with processes of inference at all. While it is true that a great deal of what is generally understood to be logic is concerned with deduction, logic, in the widest sense, refers to something far more general. It is concerned with the form of abstract structures, and is involved the moment we make pictures of reality and then seek to manipulate these pictures so that we may look further into the reality itself. It is the business of logic to invent purely artificial structures of elements and relations. Sometimes one of these structures is close enough to a real situation to be allowed to represent it. And then, because the logic is so tightly drawn, we gain insight into the reality which was previously withheld from us.[12]

The use of logical structures to represent design problems has an important consequence. It brings with it the loss of innocence. A logical picture is easier to criticize than a vague picture since the assumptions it is based on are brought out into the open. Its increased precision gives us the chance to sharpen our conception of what the design process involves. But once what we do intuitively can be described and compared with nonintuitive ways of doing the same things, we cannot go on accepting the intuitive method innocently. Whether we decide to stand for or against pure intuition as a method, we must do so for reasons which can be discussed.

I wish to state my belief in this loss of innocence very clearly, because there are many designers who are apparently not willing to accept the loss. They insist that design must be

8

a purely intuitive process: that it is hopeless to try and understand it sensibly because its problems are too deep.

There has already been one loss of innocence in the recent history of design; the discovery of machine tools to replace hand craftsmen. A century ago William Morris, the first man to see that the machines were being misused, also retreated from the loss of innocence. Instead of accepting the machine and trying to understand its implications for design, he went back to making exquisite handmade goods.[13] It was not until Gropius started his Bauhaus that designers came to terms with the machine and the loss of innocence which it entailed.[14]

Now we are at a second watershed. This time the loss of innocence is intellectual rather than mechanical. But again there are people who are trying to pretend that it has not taken place. Enormous resistance to the idea of systematic processes of design is coming from people who recognize correctly the importance of intuition, but then make a fetish of it which excludes the possibility of asking reasonable questions.

It is perhaps worth remembering that the loss of intellectual innocence was put off once before. In the eighteenth century already, certain men, Carlo Lodoli and Francesco Algarotti in Italy and the Abbé Laugier in France, no longer content to accept the formalism of the academies, began to have serious doubts about what they were doing, and raised questions of just the sort that have led, a hundred and fifty years later, to the modern revolutionary ideas on form.[15] Oddly enough, however, though these serious doubts were clearly expressed and widely read, architecture did not develop from them in the direction indicated. The doubts and questions were forgotten. Instead, in late eighteenth century Europe, we find evidence of quite another atmosphere developing, in

9

which architects based their formal invention on the rules provided by a variety of manners and "styles" like neo-Tudor, neoclassicism, chinoiserie, and neo-Gothic.[16]

It is possible to see in this course of events a desperate attempt to ward off the insecurity of selfconsciousness, and to maintain the security of innocence.

Lodoli and Laugier wanted to know what they were doing as makers of form. But the search for this knowledge only made the difficulty of their questions clear. Rather than face the responsibility of these difficult questions, designers turned instead to the authority of resurrected "styles." The architectural decisions made within a style are safe from the nagging difficulty of doubt, for the same reason that decisions are easier to make under tradition and taboo than on one's own responsibility. It is no coincidence, in my opinion, that while the Renaissance had allowed free recombinations of classical elements, the neoclassicism which replaced it stuck as closely as it could to the precise detail of Greece and Rome. By leaning on correctness, it was possible to alleviate the burden of decision. To make the secession from responsibility effective, the copy had to be exact.[17]

Now it looks as though a second secession from responsibility is taking place. It is not possible today to escape the responsibility of considered action by working within academic styles. But the designer who is unequal to his task, and unwilling to face the difficulty, preserves his innocence in other ways. The modern designer relies more and more on his position as an "artist," on catchwords, personal idiom, and intuition — for all these relieve him of some of the burden of decision, and make his cognitive problems manageable. Driven on his own resources, unable to cope with the complicated information he is supposed to organize, he hides his incompetence in a frenzy of artistic individuality. As his capacity to invent clearly conceived, well-fitting forms is exhausted further, the emphasis on intuition and individuality only grows wilder.[18]

In this atmosphere the designer's greatest gift, his intuitive ability to organize physical form, is being reduced to nothing by the size of the tasks in front of him, and mocked by the efforts of the "artists." What is worse, in an era that badly needs designers with a synthetic grasp of the organization of the physical world, the real work has to be done by less gifted engineers, because the designers hide their gift in irresponsible pretension to genius.

We must face the fact that we are on the brink of times when man may be able to magnify his intellectual and inventive capability, just as in the nineteenth century he used machines to magnify his physical capacity.[19] Again, as then, our innocence is lost. And again, of course, the innocence, once lost, cannot be regained. The loss demands attention, not denial.

PART ONE

The ultimate object of design is form.

The reason that iron filings placed in a magnetic field exhibit a pattern — or have form, as we say — is that the field they are in is not homogeneous. If the world were totally regular and homogeneous, there would be no forces, and no forms. Everything would be amorphous. But an irregular world tries to compensate for its own irregularities by fitting itself to them, and thereby takes on form.[1] D'Arcy Thompson has even called form the "diagram of forces" for the irregularities.[2] More usually we speak of these irregularities as the functional origins of the form.

The following argument is based on the assumption that physical clarity cannot be achieved in a form until there is first some programmatic clarity in the designer's mind and actions; and that for this to be possible, in turn, the designer must first trace his design problem to its earliest functional origins and be able to find some sort of pattern in them.[3] I shall try to outline a general way of stating design problems which draws attention to these functional origins, and makes their pattern reasonably easy to see.

It is based on the idea that every design problem begins with an effort to achieve fitness between two entities: the form in question and its context.[4] The form is the solution to the problem; the context defines the problem. In other words, when we speak of design, the real object of discussion is not the form alone, but the ensemble comprising the form and its context. Good fit is a desired property of this ensemble which relates to some particular division of the ensemble into form and context.[5]

There is a wide variety of ensembles which we can talk about like this. The biological ensemble made up of a natural organism and its physical environment is the most familiar: in this case we are used to describing the fit between the two as well-adaptedness.[6] But the same kind of objective aptness is to be found in many other situations. The ensemble consisting of a suit and tie is a familiar case in point; one tie goes well with a certain suit, another goes less well.[7] Again, the ensemble may be a game of chess, where at a certain stage of the game some moves are more appropriate than others because they fit the context of the previous moves more aptly.[8] The ensemble may be a musical composition — musical phrases have to fit their contexts too: think of the perfect rightness when Mozart puts just *this* phrase at a certain point in a sonata.[9] If the ensemble is a truckdriver plus a traffic sign, the graphic design of the sign must fit the demands made on it by the driver's eye. An object like a kettle has to fit the context of its use, and the technical context of its production cycle.[10] In the pursuit of urbanism, the ensemble which confronts us is the city and its habits. Here the human background which defines the need for new buildings, and the physical environment provided by the available sites, make a context for the form of the city's growth. In an extreme case of this kind, we may even speak of a culture itself as an ensemble in which the various fashions and artifacts which develop are slowly fitted to the rest.[11]

The rightness of the form depends, in each one of these cases, on the degree to which it fits the rest of the ensemble.[12]

We must also recognize that no one division of the ensemble into form and context is unique. Fitness across any one such division is just one instance of the ensemble's internal coherence. Many other divisions of the ensemble will be equally significant. Indeed, in the great majority of actual cases, it is necessary for the designer to consider several different divisions of an ensemble, superimposed, at the same time.

Let us consider an ensemble consisting of the kettle plus everything about the world outside the kettle which is relevant to the use and manufacture of household utensils. Here again there seems to be a clear boundary between the teakettle and the rest of the ensemble, if we want one, because the kettle itself is a clearly defined kind of object. But I can easily make changes in the boundary. If I say that the kettle is the wrong way to heat domestic drinking water anyway, I can quickly be involved in the redesign of the entire house, and thereby push the context back to those things outside the house which influence the house's form. Alternatively I may claim that it is not the kettle which needs to be redesigned, but the method of heating kettles. In this case the kettle becomes part of the context, while the stove perhaps is form.

There are two sides to this tendency designers have to change the definition of the problem. On the one hand, the impractical idealism of designers who want to redesign entire cities and whole processes of manufacture when they are asked to design simple objects is often only an attempt to loosen difficult constraints by stretching the form-context boundary.

On the other hand, this way in which the good designer keeps an eye on the possible changes at every point of the ensemble is part of his job. He is bound, if he knows what he is doing, to be sensitive to the fit at several boundaries within the ensemble at once. Indeed, this ability to deal with several layers of form-context boundaries in concert is an important part of what we often refer to as the designer's sense of organization. The internal coherence of an ensemble depends on a whole net of such adaptations. In a perfectly coherent ensemble we should expect the two halves of every possible division of the ensemble to fit one another.

It is true, then, that since we are ultimately interested in the ensemble as a whole, there is no good reason to divide it up just once. We ought always really to design with a number of nested, overlapped form-context boundaries in mind. Indeed, the form itself relies on its own inner organization and on the internal fitness between the pieces it is made of to control its fit as a whole to the context outside.

However, since we cannot hope to understand this highly interlaced and complex phenomenon until we understand how to achieve fit at a single arbitrarily chosen boundary, we must agree for the present to deal only with the simplest problem. Let us decide that, for the duration of any one discussion, we shall maintain the same single division of a given ensemble into form and context, even though we acknowledge that the division is probably chosen arbitrarily. And let us remember, as a corollary, that for the present we shall be giving no deep thought to the internal organization of the form as such, but only to the simplest premise and aspect of that organization: namely, that fitness which is the residue of adaptation across the single form-context boundary we choose to examine.[13]

The form is a part of the world over which we have control, and which we decide to shape while leaving the rest of the world as it is. The context is that part of the world which puts demands on this form; anything in the world that makes demands of the form is context. Fitness is a relation of mutual acceptability between these two. In a problem of design we want to satisfy the mutual demands which the two make on one another. We want to put the context and the form into effortless contact or frictionless coexistence.

We now come to the task of characterizing the fit between form and context. Let us consider a simple specific case.

It is common practice in engineering, if we wish to make a metal face perfectly smooth and level, to fit it against the surface of a standard steel block, which is level within finer limits than those we are aiming at, by inking the surface of this standard block and rubbing our metal face against the inked surface. If our metal face is not quite level, ink marks appear on it at those points which are higher than the rest. We grind away these high spots, and try to fit it against the block again. The face is level when it fits the block perfectly, so that there are no high spots which stand out any more.

This ensemble of two metal faces is so simple that we shall not be distracted by the possibility of multiple form-context boundaries within it. There is only one such boundary worth discussion at a macroscopic level, that between the standard face (the context), and the face which we are trying to smooth (the form.) Moreover, since the context is fixed, and only the form variable, the task of smoothing a metal face serves well as a paradigm design problem. In this case we may distinguish good fit from bad experimentally, by inking the standard block, putting the metal face against it, and checking the marking that gets transferred. If we wish to judge the form without actually putting it in contact with its context, in this case we may also do so. If we define levelness in mathematical terms, as a limitation on the variance which is permitted over the surface, we can test the form itself, without testing it against the context. We can do this because the criterion for levelness is, simultaneously, a description of the required form, and also a description of the context.

Consider a second, slightly more complex example. Suppose we are to invent an arrangement of iron filings which is stable when placed in a certain position in a given magnetic field. Clearly we may treat this as a design problem. The iron filings constitute a form, the magnetic field a context. Again we may easily judge the fit of a form by placing it in the magnetic field, and watching to see whether any of the filings move under its influence. If they do not, the form fits well. And again, if we wish to judge the fit of the form without recourse to this experiment, we may describe the lines of force of the magnetic field in mathematical terms, and calculate the fit or lack of fit. As before, the opportunity to evaluate the form when it is away from its context depends on the fact that we can give a precise mathematical description of the context (in this case the equations of the magnetic field).

In general, unfortunately, we cannot give an adequate description of the context we are dealing with. The fields of the contexts we encounter in the real world cannot be described in the unitary fashion we have found for levelness and magnetic fields. There is as yet no theory of ensembles capable of expressing a unitary description of the varied phenomena we encounter in the urban context of a dwelling, for example, or in a sonata, or a production cycle.

Yet we certainly need a way of evaluating the fit of a form

which does not rely on the experiment of actually trying the form out in the real world context. Trial-and-error design is an admirable method. But it is just real world trial and error which we are trying to replace by a symbolic method, because real trial and error is too expensive and too slow.

The experiment of putting a prototype form in the context itself is the real criterion of fit. A complete unitary description of the demands made by the context is the only fully adequate nonexperimental criterion. The first is too expensive, the second is impossible: so what shall we do?

Let us observe, first of all, that we should not really expect to be able to give a unitary description of the context for complex cases: if we could do so, there would be no problems of design. The context and the form are complementary. This is what lies behind D'Arcy Thompson's remark that the form is a diagram of forces.[14] Once we have the diagram of forces in the literal sense (that is, the field description of the context), this will in essence also describe the form as a complementary diagram of forces. Once we have described the levelness of the metal block, or the lines of force of the magnetic field, there is no conceptual difficulty, only a technical one, in getting the form to fit them, because the unitary description of the context is in both cases also a description of the required form.

In such cases there is no design problem. *What does make design a problem in real world cases is that we are trying to make a diagram for forces whose field we do not understand.*[15] Understanding the field of the context and inventing a form to fit it are really two aspects of the same process. It is because the context is obscure that we cannot give a direct, fully coherent criterion for the fit we are trying to achieve; and it is also its obscurity which makes the task of shaping a well-fitting form at all problematic. What do we do about this difficulty in everyday cases? Good fit means something, after all — even in cases where we cannot give a completely satisfactory fieldlike criterion for it. How is it, cognitively, that we experience the sensation of fit?

If we go back to the procedure of leveling metal faces against a standard block, and think about the way in which good fit and bad fit present themselves to us, we find a rather curious feature. Oddly enough, the procedure suggests no direct practical way of identifying good fit. We recognize bad fit whenever we see a high spot marked by ink. But in practice we see good fit only from a negative point of view, as the limiting case where there are no high spots.

Our own lives, where the distinction between good and bad fit is a normal part of everyday social behavior, show the same feature. If a man wears eighteenth-century dress today, or wears his hair down to his shoulders, or builds Gothic mansions, we very likely call his behavior odd; it does not fit our time. These are abnormalities. Yet it is such departures from the norm which stand out in our minds, rather than the norm itself. Their wrongness is somehow more immediate than the rightness of less peculiar behavior, and therefore more compelling. Thus even in everyday life the concept of good fit, though positive in meaning, seems very largely to feed on negative instances; it is the aspects of our lives which are obsolete, incongruous, or out of tune that catch our attention.

The same happens in house design. We should find it almost

impossible to characterize a house which fits its context. Yet it is the easiest thing in the world to name the specific kinds of misfit which prevent good fit. A kitchen which is hard to clean, no place to park my car, the child playing where it can be run down by someone else's car, rainwater coming in, overcrowding and lack of privacy, the eye-level grill which spits hot fat right into my eye, the gold plastic doorknob which deceives my expectations, and the front door I cannot find, are all misfits between the house and the lives and habits it is meant to fit. These misfits are the forces which must shape it, and there is no mistaking them. Because they are expressed in negative form they are specific, and tangible enough to talk about.

The same thing happens in perception. Suppose we are given a button to match, from among a box of assorted buttons. How do we proceed? We examine the buttons in the box, one at a time; but we do not look directly for a button which fits the first. What we do, actually, is to scan the buttons, rejecting each one in which we notice some discrepancy (this one is larger, this one darker, this one has too many holes, and so on), until we come to one where we can see no differences. Then we say that we have found a matching one. Notice that here again it is much easier to explain the misfit of a wrong button than to justify the congruity of one which fits.

When we speak of bad fit we refer to a single identifiable property of an ensemble, which is immediate in experience, and describable. Wherever an instance of misfit occurs in an ensemble, we are able to point specifically at what fails and to describe it. It seems as though in practice the concept of good fit, describing only the absence of such failures and hence leaving us nothing concrete to refer to in explanation, can only be explained indirectly; it is, in practice, as it were, the disjunction of all possible misfits.[16]

With this in mind, I should like to recommend that we should always expect to see the process of achieving good fit between two entities as a negative process of neutralizing the incongruities, or irritants, or forces, which cause misfit.[17]

It will be objected that to call good fit the absence of certain negative qualities is no more illuminating than to say that it is the presence of certain positive qualities.[18] However, though the two are equivalent from a logical point of view, from a phenomenological and practical point of view they are very different.[19] In practice, it will never be as natural to speak of good fit as the simultaneous satisfaction of a number of requirements, as it will be to call it the simultaneous nonoccurrence of the same number of corresponding misfits.

Let us suppose that we did try to write down a list of all possible relations between a form and its context which were required by good fit. (Such a list would in fact be just the list of requirements which designers often do try to write down.) In theory, we could then use each requirement on the list as an independent criterion, and accept a form as well fitting only if it satisfied all these criteria simultaneously.

However, thought of in this way, such a list of requirements is potentially endless, and still really needs a "field" description to tie it together. Think, for instance, of trying to specify all the properties a button had to have in order to match another. Apart from the kinds of thing we have already mentioned, size, color, number of holes, and so on, we should also have to specify its specific gravity, its electro-static charge, its viscosity, its rigidity, the fact that it should be round, that it should not be made of paper, etc., etc. In other words, we should not only have to specify the qualities which distinguish it from all other buttons, but we should also have to specify all the characteristics which actually made it a button at all.

Unfortunately, the list of distinguishable characteristics we can write down for the button is infinite. It remains infinite for all practical purposes until we discover a field description of the button. Without the field description of the button, there is no way of reducing the list of required attributes to finite terms. We are therefore forced to economize when we try to specify the nature of a matching button, because we can only grasp a finite list (and rather a short one at that). Naturally, we choose to specify those characteristics which are most likely to cause trouble in the business of matching, and which are therefore most useful in our effort to distinguish among the objects we are likely to come across in our search for buttons. But to do this, we must rely on the fact that a great many objects will not even come up for consideration. There are, after all, conceivable objects which are buttons in every respect except that they carry an electric charge of one thousand coulombs, say. Yet in practice it would be utterly superfluous, as well as rather unwieldy, to specify the electrostatic charge a well-matched button needed to have. No button we·are likely to find carries such a charge, so we ignore the possibility. The only reason we are able to match one thing with another at all is that we rely on a good deal of unexpressed information contained in the statement of the task, and take a great deal for granted.[20]

In the case of a design problem which is truly problematical, we encounter the same situation. We do not have a field description of the context, and therefore have no intrinsic way of reducing the potentially infinite set of requirements to finite terms. Yet for practical reasons we do need some way of picking a finite set from the infinite set of possible ones. In the case of requirements, no sensible way of picking this finite set presents itself. From a purely descriptive standpoint we have no way of knowing which of the infinitely many relations between form and context to include, and which ones to leave out.

But if we think of the requirements from a negative point of view, as potential misfits, there is a simple way of picking a finite set. This is because it is through misfit that the problem originally brings itself to our attention. We take just those relations between form and context which obtrude most strongly, which demand attention most clearly, which seem most likely to go wrong. We cannot do better than this.[21] If there were some intrinsic way of reducing the list of requirements to a few, this would mean in essence that we were in possession of a field description of the context: if this were so, the problem of creating fit would become trivial, and no longer a problem of design. We cannot have a unitary or field description of a context and still have a design problem worth attention.

In the case of a real design problem, even our conviction that there is such a thing as fit to be achieved is curiously flimsy and insubstantial. We are searching for some kind of harmony between two intangibles: a form which we have not yet designed, and a context which we cannot properly describe. The only reason we have for thinking that there must be some kind of fit to be achieved between them is that we can detect incongruities, or negative instances of it. The incongruities in an ensemble are the primary data of experience. If we agree to treat fit as the absence of misfits, and to use a list of those potential misfits which are most likely to occur as our criterion for fit, our theory will at least have the same nature as our intuitive conviction that there is a problem to be solved.

The results of this chapter, expressed in formal terms, are these. If we divide an ensemble into form and context, the fit between them may be regarded as an orderly condition of the ensemble, subject to disturbance in various ways, each one a potential misfit. Examples are the misfits between a house and its users, mentioned on page 23. We may summarize the state of each potential misfit by means of a binary variable. If the misfit occurs, we say the variable takes the value 1. If the misfit does not occur, we say the variable takes the value 0. Each binary variable stands for one possible kind of misfit between form and context.[22] The value this variable takes, 0 or 1, describes a state of affairs that is not either in the form alone or in the context alone, but a relation between the two. The state of this relation, fit or misfit, describes one aspect of the whole ensemble. It is a condition of harmony and good fit in the ensemble that none of the possible misfits should actually occur. We represent this fact by demanding that all the variables take the value 0.

The task of design is not to create form which meets certain conditions, but to create such an order in the ensemble that all the variables take the value 0. The form is simply that part of the ensemble over which we have control. It is only through the form that we can create order in the ensemble.

We must now try to find out how we should go about getting good fit. Where do we find it? What is the characteristic of processes which create fit successfully?

It has often been claimed in architectural circles that the houses of simpler civilizations than our own are in some sense better than our own houses.[1] While these claims have perhaps been exaggerated, the observation is still sometimes correct. I shall try to show that the facts behind it, if correctly interpreted, are of great practical consequence for an intelligently conceived process of design.

Let us consider a few famous modern houses for a moment, from the point of view of their good fit. Mies Van der Rohe's Farnsworth house, though marvelously clear, and organized under the impulse of certain tight formal rules, is certainly not a triumph economically or from the point of view of the Illinois floods.[2] Buckminster Fuller's geodesic domes have solved the weight problem of spanning space, but you can hardly put doors in them. Again, his dymaxion house, though efficient as a rapid-distribution mass-produced package, takes no account whatever of the incongruity of single free-standing houses set in the acoustic turmoil and service complexity of a modern city.[3] Even Le Corbusier in the Villa Savoie, for example, or in the Marseilles apartments, achieves his clarity

28

of form at the expense of certain elementary comforts and conveniences.[4]

Laymen like to charge sometimes that these designers have sacrificed function for the sake of clarity, because they are out of touch with the practical details of the housewife's world, and preoccupied with their own interests. This is a misleading charge. What is true is that designers do often develop one part of a functional program at the expense of another. But they do it because the only way they seem able to organize form clearly is to design under the driving force of some comparatively simple concept.

On the other hand, if designers do not aim principally at clear organization, but do try to consider all the requirements equally, we find a kind of anomaly at the other extreme. Take the average developer-built house; it is built with an eye for the market, and in a sense, therefore, fits its context well, even if superficially. But in this case the various demands made on the form are met piecemeal, without any sense of the overall organization the form needs in order to contribute as a whole to the working order of the ensemble.

Since everything in the human environment can nowadays be modified by suitable purchases at the five and ten, very little actually has to be taken care of in the house's basic organization. Instead of orienting the house carefully for sun and wind, the builder conceives its organization without concern for orientation, and light, heat, and ventilation are taken care of by fans, lamps, and other kinds of peripheral devices. Bedrooms are not separated from living rooms in plan, but are placed next to one another and the walls between them then stuffed with acoustic insulation.

The complaint that macroscopic clarity is missing in these

cases is no aesthetic whim. While it is true that an individual problem can often be solved adequately without regard for the fundamental physical order it implies, we cannot solve a whole net of such problems so casually, and get away with it. It is inconceivable that we should succeed in organizing an ensemble as complex as the modern city until we have a clear enough view of simpler design problems and their implications to produce houses which are physically clear as total organizations.

Yet at present, in our own civilization, house forms which are clearly organized and also satisfactory in all the respects demanded by the context are almost unknown.

If we look at a peasant farmhouse by comparison, or at an igloo, or at an African's mud hut, this combination of good fit and clarity is not quite so hard to find. Take the Mousgoum hut, for instance, built by African tribesmen in the northern section of the French Cameroun.[5] Apart from the variation caused by slight changes in site and occupancy, the huts vary very little. Even superficial examination shows that they are all versions of the same single form type, and convey a powerful sense of their own adequacy and nonarbitrariness.

Whether by coincidence or not, the hemispherical shape of the hut provides the most efficient surface for minimum heat transfer, and keeps the inside reasonably well protected from the heat of the equatorial sun. Its shape is maintained by a series of vertical reinforcing ribs. Besides helping to support the main fabric, these ribs also act as guides for rainwater, and are at the same time used by the builder of the hut as footholds which give him access to the upper part of the outside during its construction.[6] Instead of using disposable scaffolding (wood is very scarce), he builds the scaffolding

30

in as part of the structure. What is more, months later this "scaffolding" is still there when the owner needs to climb up on it to repair the hut. The Mousgoum cannot afford, as we do, to regard maintenance as a nuisance which is best forgotten until it is time to call the local plumber. It is in the same hands as the building operation itself, and its exigencies are as likely to shape the form as those of the initial construction.

Again, each hut nestles beautifully in the dips and hollows of the terrain. It must, because its fabric is as weak structurally as the earth it sits on, and any foreignness or discontinuity caused by careless siting would not have survived the stresses of erosion. The weather-defying concrete foundations which we rely on, and which permit the arbitrary siting of our own houses, are unknown to the Mousgoum.

The grouping of the huts reflects the social order of their inhabitants. Each man's hut is surrounded by the huts of his wives and his subservients, as social customs require — and in such a way, moreover, that these subsidiary huts also form a wall round the chief's hut and thereby protect it and themselves from wild beasts and invaders.[7]

This example shows how the pattern of the building operation, the pattern of the building's maintenance, the constraints of the surrounding conditions, and also the pattern of daily life, are fused in the form. The form has a dual coherence. It is coherently related to its context. And it is physically coherent.

This kind of dual coherence is common in simple cultures. Yet in our own culture the only forms which match these simpler forms for overall clarity of conception are those we have already mentioned, designed under the impulse of very special preoccupations. And these forms, just because they derive their clarity from simplification of the problem, fail to meet all the context's demands.[8] It is true that our functional standards are higher than those in the simple situation. It is true, and important to remember, that the simple cultures never face the problems of complexity which we face in design. And it is true that if they did face them, they would probably not make any better a showing than we do.[9] When we admire the simple situation for its good qualities, this doesn't mean that we wish we were back in the same situation. The dream of innocence is of little comfort to us; our problem, the problem of organizing form under complex constraints, is new and all our own. But in their own way the simple cultures do their simple job better than we do ours. I believe that only careful examination of their success can give us the insight we need to solve the problem of complexity. Let us ask, therefore, where this success comes from.

To answer this question we shall first have to draw a sharp and arbitrary line between those cultures we want to call simple, for the purposes of argument, and those we wish to classify with ours. I propose calling certain cultures unselfconscious, to contrast them with others, including our own, which I propose to call selfconscious.

Of course, the contrast in quality between the forms produced in the two different kinds of culture is by no means as marked as I shall suggest. Nor are the two form-making processes sharply distinguished, as my text pretends. But I have deliberately exaggerated the contrast, simply to draw attention to certain matters, important and illuminating in their own right, which we must understand before we can map out a new approach to design. It is far more important that we should understand the particular contrast I am trying to bring out, than that the facts about any given culture should be accurate or telling. This is not an anthropological treatise, and it is therefore best to think of the first part of the following discussion simply as a comparison of two descriptive constructs, the unselfconscious culture and the selfconscious culture.[10]

The cultures I choose to call "unselfconscious" have, in the past, been called by many other names — each name chosen to illuminate whatever aspect of the contrast between kinds of culture the writer was most anxious to bring out. Thus they have been called "primitive," to distinguish them from those where kinship plays a less important part in social structure;[11] "folk," to set them apart from urban cultures;[12] "closed," to draw attention to the responsibility of the individual in today's more open situation;[13] "anonymous," to distinguish them from cultures in which a profession called "architecture" exists.[14]

The particular distinction I wish to make touches only the last of these: the method of making things and buildings. Broadly, we may distinguish between our own culture, which is very selfconscious about its architecture, art, and engineering, and certain specimen cultures which are rather unselfconscious about theirs.[15] The features which distinguish architecturally unselfconscious cultures from selfconscious ones are easy to describe loosely. In the unselfconscious culture there is little thought about architecture or design as such. There is a right way to make buildings and a wrong way; but while there may be generally accepted remedies for specific failures, there are no general principles comparable to Alberti's treatises or Le Corbusier's. Since the division of labor is very

33

limited, specialization of any sort is rare, there are no architects, and each man builds his own house.[16]

The technology of communication is underdeveloped. There are no written records or architectural drawings, and little intercultural exchange. This lack of written records and lack of information about other cultures and situations means that the same experience has to be won over and over again generation after generation — without opportunity for development or change. With no variety of experience, people have no chance to see their own actions as alternatives to other possibilities, and instead of becoming selfconscious, they simply repeat the patterns of tradition, because these are the only ones they can imagine. In a word, actions are governed by habit.[17] Design decisions are made more according to custom than according to any individual's new ideas. Indeed, there is little value attached to the individual's ideas as such. There is no special market for his inventiveness. Ritual and taboo discourage innovation and self-criticism. Besides, since there is no such thing as "architecture" or "design," and no abstractly formulated problems of design, the kinds of concept needed for architectural self-criticism are too poorly developed to make such self-criticism possible; indeed the architecture itself is hardly tangibly enough conceived as such to criticize.

To be sure that such a distinction between unselfconscious and selfconscious cultures is permissible, we need a definition which will tell us whether to call a culture unselfconscious or selfconscious on the basis of visible and reportable facts alone. We find a clearly visible distinction when we look at the way the crafts of form-building are taught and learned, the institutions under which skills pass from one generation to the next.

34

For there are essentially two ways in which such education can operate, and they may be distinguished without difficulty.

At one extreme we have a kind of teaching that relies on the novice's very gradual exposure to the craft in question, on his ability to imitate by practice, on his response to sanctions, penalties, and reinforcing smiles and frowns. The great example of this kind of learning is the child's learning of elementary skills, like bicycle riding. He topples almost randomly at first, but each time he does something wrong, it fails; when he happens to do it right, its success and the fact that his success is recognized make him more likely to repeat it right.[18] Extended learning of this kind gives him a "total" feeling for the thing learned — whether it is how to ride a bicycle, or a skill like swimming, or the craft of housebuilding or weaving. The most important feature of this kind of learning is that the rules are not made explicit, but are, as it were, revealed through the correction of mistakes.[19]

The second kind of teaching tries, in some degree, to make the rules explicit. Here the novice learns much more rapidly, on the basis of general "principles." The education becomes a formal one; it relies on instruction and on teachers who train their pupils, not just by pointing out mistakes, but by inculcating positive explicit rules. A good example is lifesaving, where people rarely have the chance to learn by trial and error. In the informal situation there are no "teachers," for the novice's mistakes will be corrected by anybody who knows more than he. But in the formal situation, where learning is a specialized activity and no longer happens automatically, there are distinct "teachers" from whom the craft is learned.[20]

These teachers, or instructors, have to condense the knowledge which was once laboriously acquired in experience, for without such condensation the teaching problem would be unwieldy and unmanageable. The teacher cannot refer explicitly to each single mistake which can be made, for even if there were time to do so, such a list could not be learned. A list needs a structure for mnemonic purposes.[21] So the teacher invents teachable rules within which he accommodates as much of his unconscious training as he can — a set of shorthand principles.

In the unselfconscious culture the same form is made over and over again; in order to learn form-making, people need only learn to repeat a single familiar physical pattern. In the selfconscious culture new purposes are occurring all the time; the people who make forms are constantly required to deal with problems that are either entirely new or at best modifications of old problems. Under these circumstances it is not enough to copy old physical patterns. So that people will be able to make innovations and modifications as required, ideas about how and why things get their shape must be introduced. Teaching must be based on explicit general principles of function, rather than unmentioned and specific principles of shape.

I shall call a culture unselfconscious if its form-making is learned informally, through imitation and correction. And I shall call a culture selfconscious if its form-making is taught academically, according to explicit rules.[22]

Now why are forms made in the selfconscious culture not so well fitting or so clearly made as those in the unselfconscious culture? In one case the form-making process is a good one, in the other bad. What is it that makes a form-making process good or bad?

In explaining why the unselfconscious process is a good one, hardly anyone bothers, nowadays, to argue the myth of the primitive genius, the unsophisticated craftsman supposedly more gifted than his sophisticated counterpart.[23] The myth of architectural Darwinism has taken its place.[24] Yet though this new myth is more acceptable, in its usual form it is not really any more informative than the other.

It says, roughly, that primitive forms are good as a result of a process of gradual adaptation — that over many centuries such forms have gradually been fitted to their cultures by an intermittent though persistent series of corrections. But this explanation is vague hand-waving.[25] It doesn't tell us what it is that prevents such adaptation from taking place successfully in the selfconscious culture, which is what we want to know most urgently. And even as an explanation of good fit in the unselfconscious culture, the raw concept of adaptation is something less than satisfactory. If forms in an unselfconscious culture fit now, the chances are that they always did. We know of no outstanding differences between the present states and past states of unselfconscious cultures; and this assumption, that the fit of forms in such cultures is the result of gradual adjustment (that is, improvement) over time, does not illuminate what must actually be a dynamic process in which both form and context change continuously, and yet stay mutually well adjusted all the time.[26]

To understand the nature of the form-making process, it is not enough to give a quick one-word account of unselfconscious form-making: adaptation. We shall have to compare the detailed inner working of the unselfconscious form-making process with that of the selfconscious process, asking why one works and the other fails. Roughly speaking, I shall argue that the unselfconscious process has a structure that makes it homeostatic (self-organizing), and that it therefore consistently produces well-fitting forms, even in the face of change. And I shall argue that in a selfconscious culture the homeostatic structure of the process is broken down, so that the production of forms which fail to fit their contexts is not only possible, but likely.[27]

We decided in the last chapter that to describe fit and misfit between form and context, we must make a list of binary variables, each naming some one potential misfit which may occur.

Whether a form-making process is selfconscious or unselfconscious, these misfit variables are always present, lingering in the background of the process, as thoughts in a designer's mind, or as actions, criticisms, failures, doubts. Only the thought or the experience of possible failure provides the impetus to make new form.

At any moment in a form-making process, whether the form is in use, a prototype, as yet only a sketch, or obsolete, each of the variables is in a state of either fit or misfit. We may describe the state of all the variables at once by a row of 1's and 0's, one for each variable: for instance, for twenty variables, 0 0 1 0 0 1 1 0 1 0 1 1 1 0 1 1 0 0 0 0 would be one state. Each possible row of 1's and 0's is a possible state of the ensemble.

As form-making proceeds, so the system of variables changes state. One misfit is eradicated, another misfit occurs, and these changes in their turn set off reactions within the system that affect the states of other variables. As form and culture change, state follows state. The sequence of states which the system passes through is a record or history of the adaptation between form and context. The history of the system displays the form-making process at work. To compare unselfconscious and selfconscious form-making processes, we have only to examine the kinds of history which the system of variables can have in these two processes. As we shall see, the kinds of history which the system can have in the unselfconscious and selfconscious processes are very different.

We shall perhaps understand the idea of a system's history best if we make a simple picture of it.[28]

Imagine a system of a hundred lights. Each light can be in one of two possible states. In one state the light is on. The lights are so constructed that any light which is on always has a 50–50 chance of going off in the next second. In the other state the light is off. Connections between lights are constructed so that any light which is off has a 50–50 chance of going on again in the next second, provided at least one of the lights it is connected to is on. If the lights it is directly connected to are off, for the time being it has no chance of going on again, and stays off. If the lights are ever all off simultaneously, then they will all stay off for good, since when no light is on, none of the lights has any chance of being reactivated. This is a state of equilibrium. Sooner or later the system of lights will reach it.

This system of lights will help us understand the history of a form-making process. Each light is a binary variable, and so may be thought of as a misfit variable. The off state corresponds to fit; the on state corresponds to misfit. The fact that a light which is on has a 50–50 chance of going off every second, corresponds to the fact that whenever a misfit occurs efforts are made to correct it. The fact that lights

39

which are off can be turned on again by connected lights, corresponds to the fact that even well-fitting aspects of a form can be unhinged by changes initiated to correct some other misfit because of connections between variables. The state of equilibrium, when all the lights are off, corresponds to perfect fit or adaptation. It is the equilibrium in which all the misfit variables take the value 0. Sooner or later the system of lights will always reach this equilibrium. The only question that remains is, how long will it take for this to happen? It is not hard to see that apart from chance this depends only on the pattern of interconnections between the lights.

Let us consider two extreme circumstances.[29]

1. On the one hand, suppose there are no interconnections between lights at all. In this case there is nothing to prevent each light's staying off for good, as soon as it goes off. The average time it takes for all the lights to go off is therefore only a little greater than the average time it takes for a single light to go off, namely 2^1 seconds or 2 seconds.

2. On the other hand, imagine such rich interconnections between lights that any one light still on quickly rouses all others from the off state and puts them on again. The only way in which this system can reach adaptation is by the pure chance that all 100 happen to go off at the same moment. The average time which must elapse before this happens will be of the order of 2^{100} seconds, or 10^{22} years.

The second case is useless. The age of the universe itself is only about 10^{10} years. For all intents and purposes the system will never adapt. But the first case is no use either. In any real system there are interconnections between variables which make it impossible for each variable to adapt in complete isolation. Let us therefore construct a third possibility.

3. In this case suppose there are again interconnections among the 100 lights, but that we discern in the pattern of interconnections some 10 principal subsystems, each containing 10 lights.[30] The lights within each subsystem are so strongly connected to one another that again all 10 must go off simultaneously before they will stay off; yet at the same time the subsystems themselves are independent of one another as wholes, so that the lights in one subsystem can be switched off without being reactivated by others flashing in other subsystems. The average time it will take for all 100 lights to go off is about the same as the time it takes for one subsystem to go off, namely 2^{10} seconds, or about a quarter of an hour.

Of course, real systems do not behave so simply. But fifteen minutes is not much greater than the two seconds it takes an isolated variable to adapt, and the enormous gap between these magnitudes and 10^{22} years does teach us a vital lesson. No complex adaptive system will succeed in adapting in a reasonable amount of time unless the adaptation can proceed subsystem by subsystem, each subsystem relatively independent of the others.[31]

This is a familiar fact. It finds a close analogy in the children's sealed glass-fronted puzzles which are such fun and so infuriating. The problem, in these puzzles, is to achieve certain configurations within the box: rings on sticks, balls in sockets, pieces of various shapes in odd-shaped frames — but all to be done by gentle tapping on the outside of the box. Think of the simplest of these puzzles, where half a dozen colored beads, say, are each to be put in a hole of corresponding color.

One way to go about this problem would be to pick the

puzzle up, give it a single energetic shake, and lay it down again, in the hope that the correct configuration would appear by accident. This all-or-nothing method might be repeated many thousand times, but it is clear that its chances of success are negligible. It is the technique of a child who does not understand how best to play. Much the easiest way — and the way we do in fact adopt under such circumstances — is to juggle one bead at a time. Once a bead is in, provided we tap gently, it is in for good, and we are free to manipulate the next one that presents itself, and we achieve the full configuration step by step. When we treat each bead as an isolable subsystem, and take the subsystems independently, we can solve the puzzle.

If we now consider the process of form-making, in the light of these examples, we see an easy way to make explicit the distinction between processes which work and those which don't.

Let us remind ourselves of the precise sense in which there is a system active in a form-making process. It is a purely fictitious system. Its variables are the conditions which must be met by good fit between form and context. Its interactions are the causal linkages which connect the variables to one another. If there is not enough light in a house, for instance, and more windows are added to correct this failure, the change may improve the light but allow too little privacy; another change for more light makes the windows bigger, perhaps, but thereby makes the house more likely to collapse. These are examples of inter-variable linkage. If we represent this system by drawing a point for each misfit variable, and a link between two points for each such causal linkage, we get a structure which looks something like this:

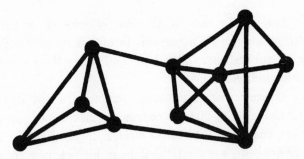

Now, let us go back to the question of adaptation. Clearly these misfit variables, being interconnected, cannot adjust independently, one by one. On the other hand, since not all the variables are equally strongly connected (in other words there are not only dependences among the variables, but also *independences*), there will always be subsystems like those circled below, which can, in principle, operate fairly independently.[32]

We may therefore picture the process of form-making as the action of a series of subsystems, all interlinked, yet sufficiently free of one another to adjust independently in a feasible amount of time. It works, because the cycles of correction and recorrection, which occur during adaptation, are restricted to one subsystem at a time.

We shall not be able to see, directly, whether or not the unselfconscious and selfconscious form-making processes operate by subsystems. Instead we shall infer their modes of operation indirectly.

The greatest clue to the inner structure of any dynamic process lies in its reaction to change. A culture does not move from one change to the next in discrete steps, of course. New threads are being woven all the time, making changes continuous and smooth. But from the point of view of its effect on a form, change only becomes significant at that moment when a failure or misfit reaches critical importance — at that moment when it is recognized, and people feel the form has something wrong with it. It is therefore legitimate, for our purpose, to consider a culture as changing in discrete steps.[33]

We wish to know, now, how the form-making process reacts to one such change. Whether a new, previously unknown misfit occurs or a known one recurs, in both cases, from our point of view, some one variable changes value from 0 to 1. What, precisely, happens when a misfit variable takes the value 1? How does the process behave under this stimulus?

Let us go back for a moment to our system of 100 lights. Suppose the system is in a state of fit — that is, all the lights are switched off. Now imagine that every once in a while one light gets switched on by an outside agent, even though no others are on to activate it. By waiting to see what happens next, we can very easily deduce the inner nature of the system, even though we cannot see it directly. If the light always flashes just once, and then goes off again and stays off, we deduce that the lights are able to adapt independently, and hence that there are no interconnections between lights. If the light activates a few other lights, and they flash together

44

for a while, and then switch themselves off, we deduce that there are subsystems of interconnected lights active. If the light flashes and then activates other lights until all of them are flashing, and they never settle down again, we deduce that the system is unable to adapt subsystem by subsystem because the interconnections are too rich.

The solitary light switched on by an external agent is the occasional misfit which occurs. The reaction of the system to the disturbance is the reaction of the form-making process to the misfit. If we detect the active presence of subsystems in a process, we may then argue (by induction, as it were) that this is fully responsible for the good fit of the forms being produced by the process. For if good forms can always be adjusted correctly the moment any slight misfit occurs, then no sequence of changes will destroy the good fit ever (at least while the process maintains this character); and provided there was good fit at some stage in the past, no matter how remote (the first term of the induction), it will have persisted, because there is an active stability at work.[34] If, on the other hand, a form-making process is such that a minor culture change can upset the good fit of the forms it produces, then any well-fitting forms we may observe at one time or another fit only by accident; and the next cultural deflection may once more lead to the production of badly fitting forms.

It is the inner nature of the process which counts. The vital point that underlies the following discussion is that the form-builders in unselfconscious cultures respond to small changes in a way that allows the subsystems of the misfit system to work independently — but that because the selfconscious response to change cannot take place subsystem by subsystem, its forms are arbitrary.

Let us turn our attention, first of all, to the unselfconscious cultures. It will be necessary first to outline the conditions under which forms in unselfconscious cultures are produced. We know by definition that building skills are learned informally, without the help of formulated rules.[1] However, although there are no formulated rules (or perhaps indeed, as we shall see later, just because there are none), the unspoken rules are of great complexity, and are rigidly maintained. There is a way to do things, a way not to do them. There is a firmly set tradition, accepted beyond question by all builders of form, and this tradition strongly resists change.

The existence of such powerful traditions, and evidence of their rigidity, already are shown to some extent in those aspects of unselfconscious cultures which have been discussed. It is clear, for instance, that forms do not remain the same for centuries without traditions springing up about them. If the Egyptian houses of the Nile have the same plan now as the houses whose plans were pictured in the hieroglyphs,[2] we can be fairly certain that their makers are in the grip of a tradition. Anywhere where forms are virtually the same now as they were thousands of years ago, the bonds must be extremely strong. In southern Italy, neither the *trulli* of Apulia nor the coalburners' *capanne* of Anzio near Rome have changed since prehistoric times.[3] The same is known to be true of the black houses of the Outer Hebrides, and of the hogans of the Navaho.[4]

The most visible feature of architectural tradition in such unselfconscious cultures is the wealth of myth and legend attached to building habits. While the stories rarely deal exclusively with dwellings, nevertheless descriptions of the house, its form, its origins, are woven into many of the global myths which lie at the very root of culture; and wherever this occurs, not only is the architectural tradition made unassailable, but its constant repetition is assured. The black tents, for example, common among nomads from Tunisia to Afghanistan, figure more than once in the Old Testament.[5] In a similar way the folk tales of old Ireland and the Outer Hebrides are full of oblique references to the shape of houses.[6] The age of these examples gives us an inkling of the age and strength of the traditions which maintain the shape of unselfconscious dwelling forms. Wherever the house is mentioned in a myth or lore, it at once becomes part of the higher order, ineffable, immutable, not to be changed. When certain Indians of the Amazon believe that after death the soul retires to a house at the source of a mysterious river,[7] the mere association of the house with a story of this kind discourages all thoughtful criticism of the standard form, and sets its "rightness" well beyond the bounds of question.

More forceful still, of course, are rituals and taboos connected with the dwelling. Throughout Polynesia the resistance to change makes itself felt quite unequivocally in the fact that the building of a house is a ceremonial occasion.[8] The performance of the priests, and of the workers, though different from one island to the next, is always clearly speci-

47

fied; and the rigidity of these behavior patterns, by preserving techniques, preserves the forms themselves and makes change extremely difficult. The Navaho Indians, too, make their hogans the center of the most elaborate performance.[9] Again the gravity of the rituals, and their rigidity, make it impossible that the form of the hogan should be lightly changed.

The rigidity of tradition is at its clearest, though, in the case where builders of form are forced to work within definitely given limitations. The Samoan, if he is to make a good house, must use wood from the breadfruit tree.[10] The Italian peasant making his *trullo* at Alberobello is allowed latitude for individual expression only in the lump of plaster which crowns the cone of the roof.[11] The Wanoe has a chant which tells him precisely the sequence of operations he is to follow while building his house.[12] The Welshman must make the crucks which support his roof precisely according to the pattern of tradition.[13] The Sumatran gives his roofs their special shape, not because this is structurally essential, but because this is the way to make roofs in Sumatra.[14]

Every one of these examples points in the same direction. Unselfconscious cultures contain, as a feature of their form-producing systems, a certain built-in fixity — patterns of myth, tradition, and taboo which resist willful change. Form-builders will only introduce changes under strong compulsion where there are powerful (and obvious) irritations in the existing forms which demand correction.

Now when there are such irritations, how fast does the failure lead to action, how quickly does it lead to a change of form? Think first, perhaps, of man's closeness to the ground in the unselfconscious culture, and of the materials he uses when

48

he makes his house. The Hebridean crofter uses stone and clay and sods and grass and straw, all from the near surroundings.[15] The Indian's tent used to be made of hide from the buffalo he ate.[16] The Apulian uses as building stones the very rocks which he has taken from the ground to make his agriculture possible.[17] These men have a highly developed eye for the trees and stones and animals which contain the means of their livelihood, their food, their medicine, their furniture, their tools. To an African tribesman the materials available are not simply objects, but are full of life.[18] He knows them through and through; and they are always close to hand.

Closely associated with this immediacy is the fact that the owner is his own builder, that the form-maker not only makes the form but lives in it. Indeed, not only is the man who lives in the form the one who made it, but there is a special closeness of contact between man and form which leads to constant rearrangement of unsatisfactory detail, constant improvement. The man, already responsible for the original shaping of the form, is also alive to its demands while he inhabits it.[19] And anything which needs to be changed is changed at once.

The Abipon, whose dwelling was the simplest tent made of two poles and a mat, dug a trench to carry off the rain if it bothered him.[20] The Eskimo reacts constantly to every change in temperature inside the igloo by opening holes or closing them with lumps of snow.[21] The very special directness of these actions may be made clearer, possibly, as follows. Think of the moment when the melting snow dripping from the roof is no longer bearable, and the man goes to do something about it. He makes a hole which lets some cold air in, perhaps. The man realizes that he has to do something about it — but he does not do so by remembering the general rule and then applying it ("When the snow starts to melt it is too hot inside the igloo and therefore time to . . ."). He simply does it. And though words may accompany his action, they play no essential part in it. This is the important point. The failure or inadequacy of the form leads directly to the action.

This directness is the second crucial feature of the unselfconscious system's form-production. Failure and correction go side by side. There is no deliberation in between the recognition of a failure and the reaction to it.[22] The directness is enhanced, too, by the fact that building and repair are so much an everyday affair. The Eskimo, on winter hunts, makes a new igloo every night.[23] The Indian's tepee cover rarely lasts more than a single season.[24] The mud walls of the Tallensi hut need frequent daubs.[25] Even the elaborate communal dwellings of the Amazon tribes are abandoned every two or three years, and new ones built.[26] Impermanent materials and unsettled ways of life demand constant reconstruction and repair, with the result that the shaping of form is a task perpetually before the dweller's eyes and hands. If a form is made the same way several times over, or even simply left unchanged, we can be fairly sure that its inhabitant finds little wrong with it. Since its materials are close to hand, and their use his own responsibility, he will not hesitate to act if there are any minor changes which seem worth making.

Let us return now to the question of adaptation. The basic principle of adaptation depends on the simple fact that the process toward equilibrium is irreversible. Misfit provides an incentive to change; good fit provides none. In theory the process is eventually bound to reach the equilibrium of well-fitting forms.

However, for the fit to occur in practice, one vital condition must be satisfied. It must have time to happen. The process must be able to achieve its equilibrium before the next culture change upsets it again. It must actually have time to reach its equilibrium every time it is disturbed — or, if we see the process as continuous rather than intermittent, the adjustment of forms must proceed more quickly than the drift of the culture context. Unless this condition is fulfilled the system can never produce well-fitting forms, for the equilibrium of the adaptation will not be sustained.

As we saw in Chapter 3, the speed of adaptation depends essentially on whether the adaptation can take place in independent and restricted subsystems, or not. Although we cannot actually see these subsystems in the unselfconscious process, we can infer their activity from the very two characteristics of the process which we have been discussing: directness and tradition.

The direct response is the feedback of the process.[27] If the process is to maintain the good fit of dwelling forms while the culture drifts, it needs a feedback sensitive enough to take action the moment that one of the potential failures actually occurs. The vital feature of the feedback is its immediacy. For only through prompt action can it prevent the build-up of multiple failures which would then demand simultaneous correction — a task which might, as we have seen, take too long to be feasible in practice.

However, the sensitivity of feedback is not in itself enough to lead to equilibrium. The feedback must be controlled, or damped, somehow.[28] Such control is provided by the resistance to change the unselfconscious culture has built into its traditions. We might say of these traditions, possibly, that they make the system viscous. This viscosity damps the changes

5 1

made, and prevents their extension to other aspects of the form. As a result only urgent changes are allowed. Once a form fits well, changes are not made again until it fails to fit again. Without this action of tradition, the repercussions and ripples started by the slightest failure could grow wider and wider until they were spreading too fast to be corrected.

On the one hand the directness of the response to misfit ensures that each failure is corrected as soon as it occurs, and thereby restricts the change to one subsystem at a time. And on the other hand the force of tradition, by resisting needless change, holds steady all the variables not in the relevant subsystem, and prevents those minor disturbances outside the subsystem from taking hold. Rigid tradition and immediate action may seem contradictory. But it is the very contrast between these two which makes the process self-adjusting. It is just the fast reaction to single failures, complemented by resistance to all other change, which allows the process to make series of minor adjustments instead of spasmodic global ones: it is able to adjust subsystem by subsystem, so that the process of adjustment is faster than the rate at which the culture changes; equilibrium is certain to be re-established whenever slight disturbances occur; and the forms are not simply well-fitted to their cultures, but in active equilibrium with them.[29]

The operation of such a process hardly taxes the individual craftsman's ability at all. The man who makes the form is an agent simply, and very little is required of him during the form's development. Even the most aimless changes will eventually lead to well-fitting forms, because of the tendency to equilibrium inherent in the organization of the process.

All the agent need do is to recognize failures when they occur, and to react to them. And this even the simplest man can do. For although only few men have sufficient integrative ability to invent form of any clarity, we are all able to criticize existing forms.[30] It is especially important to understand that the agent in such a process needs no creative strength. He does not need to be able to improve the form, only to make some sort of change when he notices a failure. The changes may not be always for the better; but it is not necessary that they should be, since the operation of the process allows only the improvements to persist.

To make the foregoing analysis quite clear, I shall use it to illuminate a rather curious phenomenon.[31] The Slovakian peasants used to be famous for the shawls they made. These shawls were wonderfully colored and patterned, woven of yarns which had been dipped in homemade dyes. Early in the twentieth century aniline dyes were made available to them. And at once the glory of the shawls was spoiled; they were now no longer delicate and subtle, but crude. This change cannot have come about because the new dyes were somehow inferior. They were as brilliant, and the variety of colors was much greater than before. Yet somehow the new shawls turned out vulgar and uninteresting.

Now if, as it is so pleasant to suppose, the shawlmakers had had some innate artistry, had been so gifted that they were simply "able" to make beautiful shawls, it would be almost impossible to explain their later clumsiness. But if we look at the situation differently, it is very easy to explain. The shawlmakers were simply able, as many of us are, to recognize *bad* shawls, and their own mistakes.

Over the generations the shawls had doubtless often been

made extremely badly. But whenever a bad one was made, it was recognized as such, and therefore not repeated. And though nothing is to say that the change made would be for the better, it would still be a change. When the results of such changes were still bad, further changes would be made. The changes would go on until the shawls were good. And only at this point would the incentive to go on changing the patterns disappear.

So we do not need to pretend that these craftsmen had special ability. They made beautiful shawls by standing in a long tradition, and by making minor changes whenever something seemed to need improvement. But once presented with more complicated choices, their apparent mastery and judgment disappeared. Faced with the complex unfamiliar task of actually inventing forms from scratch, they were unsuccessful.

In the unselfconscious culture a clear pattern has emerged. Being self-adjusting, its action allows the production of well-fitting forms to persist in active equilibrium with the system.

The way forms are made in the selfconscious culture is very different. I shall try to show how, just as it is a property of the unselfconscious system's organization that it produces well-fitting forms, so it is a property of the emergent self-conscious system that its forms fit badly.

In one way it is easy enough to see what goes wrong with the arrival of selfconsciousness. The very features which we have found responsible for stability in the unselfconscious process begin to disappear.

The reaction to failure, once so direct, now becomes less and less direct. Materials are no longer close to hand. Buildings are more permanent, frequent repair and readjustment less common, than they used to be. Construction is no longer in the hands of the inhabitants; failures, when they occur, have to be several times reported and described before the specialist will recognize them and make some permanent adjustment. Each of these changes blunts the hair-fine sensitivity of the unselfconscious process' response to failure, so that failures now need to be quite considerable before they will induce correction.

55

The firmness of tradition too, dissolves. The resistance to willful change weakens, and change for its own sake becomes acceptable. Instead of forms being held constant in all respects but one, so that correction can be immediately effective, the interplay of simultaneous changes is now uncontrolled. To put it playfully, the viscosity which brought the unselfconscious process to rest when there were no failures left, is thinned by the high temperature of selfconsciousness. And as a result the system's drive to equilibrium is no longer irreversible; any equilibrium the system finds will not now be sustained; those aspects of the process which could sustain it have dropped away.

In any case, the culture that once was slow-moving, and allowed ample time for adaptation, now changes so rapidly that adaptation cannot keep up with it. No sooner is adjustment of one kind begun than the culture takes a further turn and forces the adjustment in a new direction. No adjustment is ever finished. And the essential condition on the process — that it should in fact have time to reach its equilibrium — is violated.

This has all actually happened. In our own civilization, the process of adaptation and selection which we have seen at work in unselfconscious cultures has plainly disappeared. But that is not in itself enough to account for the fact that the selfconscious culture does not manage to produce clearly organized, well-fitting forms in its own way. Though we may easily be right in putting our present unsuccess down to our selfconsciousness, we must find out just what it is about selfconscious form-production that causes trouble. The pathology of the selfconscious culture is puzzling in its own right, and is not to be explained simply by the passing of the unselfconscious process.

I do not wish to imply here that there is any unique process of development that makes selfconscious cultures out of unselfconscious ones. Let us remember anyway that the distinction between the two is artificial. And, besides, the facts of history suggest that the development from one to the other can happen in rather different ways.[1] From the point of view of my present argument it is immaterial how the development occurs. All that matters, actually, is that sooner or later the phenomenon of the master craftsman takes control of the form-making activities.

One example, of an early kind, of developing selfconsciousness is found in Samoa. Although ordinary Samoan houses are built by their inhabitants-to-be, custom demands that guest houses be built exclusively by carpenters.[2] Since these carpenters need to find clients, they are in business as artists; and they begin to make personal innovations and changes for no reason except that prospective clients will judge their work for its inventiveness.[3]

The form-maker's assertion of his individuality is an important feature of selfconsciousness. Think of the willful forms of our own limelight-bound architects. The individual, since his livelihood depends on the reputation he achieves, is anxious to distinguish himself from his fellow architects, to make innovations, and to be a star.[4]

The development of architectural individualism is the clearest manifestation of the moment when architecture first turns into a selfconscious discipline. And the selfconscious architect's individualism is not entirely willful either. It is a natural consequence of a man's decision to devote his life exclusively to the one activity called "architecture."[5] Clearly it is at this stage too that the activity first becomes ripe for serious thought and theory. Then, with architecture once established as a discipline, and the individual architect established, entire institutions are soon devoted exclusively to the study and development of design. The academies are formed. As the academies develop, the unformulated precepts of tradition give way to clearly formulated concepts whose very formulation invites criticism and debate.[6] Question leads to unrest, architectural freedom to further selfconsciousness, until it turns out that (for the moment anyway) the form-maker's freedom has been dearly bought. For the discovery of architecture as an independent discipline costs the form-making process many fundamental changes. Indeed, in the sense I shall now try to describe, architecture did actually fail from the very moment of its inception. With the invention of a teachable discipline called "architecture," the old process of making form was adulterated and its chances of success destroyed.

The source of this trouble lies with the individual. In the unselfconscious system the individual is no more than an agent.[7] He does what he knows how to do as best he can. Very little demand is made of him. He need not himself be able to invent forms at all. All that is required is that he should recognize misfits and respond to them by making minor changes. It is not even necessary that these changes be for the better. As we have seen, the system, being self-adjusting, finds its own equilibrium — provided only that misfit incites *some* reaction in the craftsman. The forms produced in such a system are not the work of individuals, and their success does not depend on any one man's artistry, but only on the artist's place within the process.[8]

The selfconscious process is different. The artist's self-conscious recognition of his individuality has deep effect on the process of form-making. Each form is now seen as the work of a single man, and its success is his achievement only. Selfconsciousness brings with it the desire to break loose, the taste for individual expression, the escape from tradition and taboo, the will to self-determination. But the wildness of the desire is tempered by man's limited invention. To achieve in a few hours at the drawing board what once took centuries of adaptation and development, to invent a form suddenly which clearly fits its context — the extent of the invention necessary is beyond the average designer.

A man who sets out to achieve this adaptation in a single leap is not unlike the child who shakes his glass-topped puzzle fretfully, expecting at one shake to arrange the bits inside correctly.[9] The designer's attempt is hardly random as the child's is; but the difficulties are the same. *His chances of success are small because the number of factors which must fall simultaneously into place is so enormous.*

Now, in a sense, the limited capacity of the individual designer makes further treatment of the failure of selfconsciousness superfluous. If the selfconscious culture relies on the individual to produce its forms, and the individual isn't up to it, there seems nothing more to say. But it is not so simple. The individual is not merely weak. The moment he becomes aware of his own weakness in the face of the enormous challenge of a new design problem, he takes steps to overcome his weakness; and strangely enough these steps themselves exert a very positive bad influence on the way he develops forms. In fact, we shall see that the selfconscious system's lack of success really doesn't lie so much in the individual's lack of capacity as in the kind of efforts he makes, when he is selfconscious, to overcome this incapacity.

Let us look again at just what kind of difficulty the designer faces. Take, for example, the design of a simple kettle. He has to invent a kettle which fits the context of its use. It must not be too small. It must not be hard to pick up when it is hot. It must not be easy to let go of by mistake. It must not be hard to store in the kitchen. It must not be hard to get the water out of. It must pour cleanly. It must not let the water in it cool too quickly. The material it is made of must not cost too much. It must be able to withstand the temperature of boiling water. It must not be too hard to clean on the outside. It must not be a shape which is too hard to machine. It must not be a shape which is unsuitable for whatever reasonably priced metal it is made of. It must not be too hard to assemble, since this costs man-hours of labor. It must not corrode in steamy kitchens. Its inside must not be too difficult to keep free of scale. It must not be hard to fill with water. It must not be uneconomical to heat small quantities of water in, when it is not full. It must not appeal to such a minority that it cannot be manufactured in an appropriate way because of its small demand. It must not be so tricky to hold that accidents occur when children or invalids try to use it. It must not be able to boil dry and burn out without warning. It must not be unstable on the stove while it is boiling.

I have deliberately filled a page with the list of these twenty-one detailed requirements or misfit variables so as to bring home the amorphous nature of design problems as they present themselves to the designer. Naturally the design of a complex object like a motor car is much more difficult and requires a much longer list. It is hardly necessary to speculate as to the length and apparent disorder of a list which could adequately define the problem of designing a complete urban environment.

How is a designer to deal with this highly amorphous and diffuse condition of the problem as it confronts him? What would any of us do?

Since we cannot refer to the list in full each time we think about the problem, we invent a shorthand notation. We classify the items, and then think about the names of the classes: since there are fewer of these, we can think about them much more easily. To put it in the language of psychology, there are limits on the number of distinct concepts which we can manipulate cognitively at any one time, and we are therefore forced, if we wish to get a view of the whole problem, to re-encode these items.[10] Thus, in the case of the kettle, we might think about the class of requirements generated by the process of the kettle's manufacture, its capacity, its safety requirements, the economics of heating water, and its good looks. Each of these concepts is a general name for a number of the specific requirements. If we were in a very great hurry (or for some reason wanted to simplify the problem even further), we might even classify these concepts in turn, and deal with the problem simply in terms of (1) its function and (2) its economics. In this case we would have erected a four-level hierarchy like that in the diagram on the next page.

By erecting such a hierarchy of concepts for himself, the

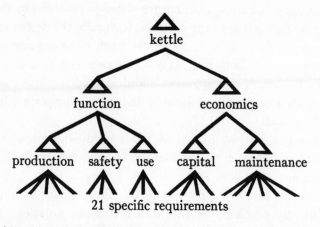

21 specific requirements

designer is, after all, able to face the problem all at once. He achieves a powerful economy of thought, and can by this means thread his way through far more difficult problems than he could cope with otherwise. If hierarchies seem less common in practice than I seem to suggest, we have only to look at the contents of any engineering manual or architects' catalogue; the hierarchy of chapter headings and subheadings is organized the way it is, precisely for cognitive convenience.[11]

To help himself overcome the difficulties of complexity, the designer tries to organize his problem. He classifies its various aspects, thereby gives it shape, and makes it easier to handle. What bothers him is not only the difficulty of the problem either. The constant burden of decision which he comes across, once freed from tradition, is a tiring one. So he avoids it where he can by using rules (or general principles), which he formulates in terms of his invented concepts. These principles are at the root of all so-called "theories" of architectural design.[12] They are prescriptions which relieve the burden of selfconsciousness and of too much responsibility.

It is rash, perhaps, to call the invention of either concepts or prescriptions a conscious attempt to simplify problems. In practice they unfold as the natural outcome of critical discussion about design. In other words, the generation of verbal concepts and rules need not only be seen abstractly as the supposed result of the individual's predicament, but may be observed wherever the kind of formal education we have called selfconscious occurs.

A novice in the unselfconscious situation learns by being put right whenever he goes wrong. "No, not that way, this way." No attempt is made to formulate abstractly just what the right way involves. The right way is the residue when all the wrong ways are eradicated. But in an intellectual atmosphere free from the inhibition of tradition, the picture changes. The moment the student is free to question what he is told, and value is put on explanation, it becomes important to decide why "this" is the right way rather than "that," and to look for general reasons. Attempts are made to aggregate the specific failures and successes which occur, into principles. And each such general principle now takes the place of many separate and specific admonitions. It tells us to avoid this kind of form, perhaps, or praises that kind. With failure and success defined, the training of the architect develops rapidly. The huge list of specific misfits which can occur, too complex for the student to absorb abstractly and for that reason usually to be grasped only through direct experience, as it is in the unselfconscious culture, *can* now be learned — because it has been given form. The misfit variables are patterned into categories like "economics" or "acoustics." And condensed, like this, they can be taught, discussed, and criticized. It is this point, where these concept-determined principles begin to figure in the training and practice of the architect, that the ill-effect of selfconsciousness on form begins to show itself.

I shall now try to draw attention to the peculiar and damaging arbitrariness of the concepts which are invented. Let us remember that the system of interdependent requirements or misfit variables active in the unselfconscious ensemble is still present underneath the surface.

Suppose, as before, we picture the system crudely by drawing a link between every pair of interdependent requirements: we get something that looks like this.

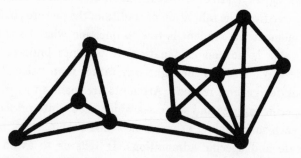

As we have seen before, the variables of such a system can be adjusted to meet the specified conditions in a reasonable time only if its subsystems are adjusted independently of one another. A subsystem, roughly speaking, is one of the obvious components of the system, like the parts shown with a circle round them. If we try to adjust a set of variables which does not constitute a subsystem, the repercussions of the adjustment affect others outside the set, because the set is not sufficiently independent. What we saw in Chapter 4, effectively, was that the procedure of the unselfconscious system is so

organized that adjustment *can* take place in each one of these subsystems independently. This is the reason for its success.

In the selfconscious situation, on the other hand, the designer is faced with all the variables simultaneously. Yet we know from the simple computation on page 40 that if he tries to manipulate them all at once he will not manage to find a well-fitting form in any reasonable time. When he himself senses this difficulty, he tries to break the problem down, and so invents concepts to help himself decide which subsets of requirements to deal with independently. Now what are these concepts, in terms of the system of variables? Each concept identifies a certain collection of the variables. "Economics" identifies one part of the system, "safety" another, "acoustics" another, and so on.

My contention is this. These concepts will not help the designer in finding a well-adapted solution unless they happen to correspond to the system's subsystems. But since the concepts are on the whole the result of arbitrary historical accidents, there is no reason to expect that they will in fact correspond to these subsystems. They are just as likely to identify any other parts of the system, like this:

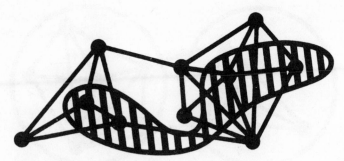

Of course this demonstrates only that concepts *can* easily be arbitrary. It does not show that the concepts used in practice actually are so. Indeed, clearly, their arbitrariness can only be established for individual and specific cases. Detailed analysis of the problem of designing urban family houses, for instance, has shown that the usually accepted functional categories like acoustics, circulation, and accommodation are inappropriate for this problem.[13] Similarly, the principle of the "neighborhood," one of the old chestnuts of city-planning theory, has been shown to be an inadequate mental component of the residential planning problem.[14] But since such demonstrations can only be made for special cases, let us examine a more general, rather plausible reason for believing that such verbal concepts always will be of this arbitrary kind.

Every concept can be defined and understood in two complementary ways. We may think of it as the name of a class of objects or subsidiary concepts; or we may think of what it means. We define a concept *in extension* when we specify all the elements of the class it refers to. And we define a concept *in intension* when we try to explain its meaning analytically in terms of other concepts at the same level.[15]

66

For the sake of argument I have just been treating terms like "acoustics" as class names, as a collective way of talking about a number of more specific requirements. The "neighborhood," too, though less abstract and more physical, is still a concept which summarizes mentally all those specific requirements, like primary schooling, pedestrian safety, and community, which a physical neighborhood is supposed to meet. In other words, each of the concepts "acoustics" and "neighborhood" is a variable whose value extension is the same as that given by the conjunction of all the value extensions of the specific acoustic variables, or the specific community-living variables, respectively.[16] This extensional view of the concept is convenient for the sake of mathematical clarity. But in practice, as a rule, concepts are not generated or defined in extension; they are generated in intension. That is, we fit new concepts into the pattern of everyday language by relating their meanings to those of other words at present available in English.

Yet this part played by language in the invention of new concepts, though very important from the point of view of communication and understanding, is almost entirely irrelevant from the point of view of a problem's structure.[17] The demand that a new concept be definable and comprehensible is important from the point of view of teaching and self-conscious design. Take the concept "safety," for example. Its existence as a common word is convenient and helps hammer home the very general importance of keeping designs danger-free. But it is used in the statement of such dissimilar problems as the design of a tea kettle and the design of a highway interchange. As far as its meaning is concerned it is relevant to both. But as far as the individual structure of the two problems goes, it seems unlikely that the one word should successfully identify a principal component subsystem in each of these two very dissimilar problems. Unfortunately, although every problem has its own structure, and there are many different problems, the words we have available to describe the components of these problems are generated by forces in the language, not by the problems, and are therefore rather limited in number and cannot describe more than a few cases correctly.[18]

Take the simple problem of the kettle. I have listed 21 requirements which must take values within specified limits in an acceptably designed kettle. Given a set of n things, there are 2^n different subsets of these things. This means that there are 2^{21} distinct subsets of variables any one of which may possibly be an important component subsystem of the kettle problem. To name each of these components alone we should already need more than a million different words — more than there are in the English language.

A designer may object that his thinking is never as verbal as I have implied, and that, instead of using verbal concepts, he prepares himself for a complicated problem by making diagrams of its various aspects. This is true. Let us remember, however, just what things a designer tries to diagram. Physical concepts like "neighborhood" or "circulation pattern" have no more universal validity than verbal concepts. They are still bound by the conceptual habits of the draftsman. A typical sequence of diagrams which precede an architectural problem will include a circulation diagram, a diagram of acoustics, a diagram of the load-bearing structure, a diagram of sun and wind perhaps, a diagram of the social neighborhoods. I maintain that these diagrams are used only because

68

the principles which define them — acoustics, circulation, weather, neighborhood — happen to be part of current architectural usage, not because they bear a well-understood fundamental relation to any particular problem being investigated.[19]

As it stands, the selfconscious design procedure provides no structural correspondence between the problem and the means devised for solving it. The complexity of the problem is never fully disentangled, and the forms produced not only fail to meet their specifications as fully as they should, but also lack the formal clarity which they would have if the organization of the problem they are fitted to were better understood.

It is perhaps worth adding, as a footnote, a slightly different angle on the same difficulty. The arbitrariness of the existing verbal concepts is not their only disadvantage, for once they are invented, verbal concepts have a further ill-effect on us. We lose the ability to modify them. In the unselfconscious situation the action of culture on form is a very subtle business, made up of many minute concrete influences. But once these concrete influences are represented symbolically in verbal terms, and these symbolic representations or names subsumed under larger and still more abstract categories to make them amenable to thought, they begin seriously to impair our ability to see beyond them.[20]

Where a number of issues are being taken into account in a design decision, inevitably the ones which can be most clearly expressed carry the greatest weight, and are best reflected in the form. Other factors, important too but less well expressed, are not so well reflected. Caught in a net of language of our own invention, we overestimate the language's impartiality. Each concept, at the time of its invention no more than a concise way of grasping many issues, quickly becomes a precept. We take the step from description to criterion too easily, so that what is at first a useful tool becomes a bigoted preoccupation.

The Roman bias toward functionalism and engineering did not reach its peak until after Vitruvius had formulated the functionalist doctrine.[21] The Parthenon could only have been created during a time of preoccupation with aesthetic problems, after the earlier Greek invention of the concept "beauty." England's nineteenth century low-cost slums were conceived only after monetary values had explicitly been given great importance through the concept "economics," invented not long before.[22]

In this fashion the selfconscious individual's grasp of problems is constantly misled. His concepts and categories, besides being arbitrary and unsuitable, are self-perpetuating. Under the influence of concepts, he not only does things from a biased point of view, but sees them biasedly as well. The concepts control his perception of fit and misfit — until in the end he sees nothing but deviations from his conceptual dogmas, and loses not only the urge but even the mental opportunity to frame his problems more appropriately.

PART TWO

Here is the problem. We wish to design clearly conceived forms which are well adapted to some given context. We have seen that for this to be feasible, the adaptation must take place independently within independent subsystems of variables. In the unselfconscious situation this occurs automatically, because the individual craftsman has too little control over the process to upset the pattern of adaptation implicit in the ensemble. Unfortunately this situation no longer exists; the number of variables has increased, the information confronting us is profuse and confusing, and our attempts to duplicate the natural organization of the unselfconscious process selfconsciously are thwarted, because the very thoughts we have, as we try to help ourselves, distort the problem and make it too unclear to solve.

The dilemma is simple. As time goes on the designer gets more and more control over the process of design. But as he does so, his efforts to deal with the increasing cognitive burden actually make it harder and harder for the real causal structure of the problem to express itself in this process.

What can we do to overcome this difficulty? On the face of it, it is hard to see how any systematic theory can ease it much. There are certain kinds of problems, like some of those that occur in economics, checkers, logic, or administration, which can be clarified and solved mechanically.[1] They can be solved mechanically, because they are well enough understood for us to turn them into selection problems.[2]

To solve a problem by selection, two things are necessary.

1. It must be possible to generate a wide enough range of possible alternative solutions symbolically.
2. It must be possible to express all the criteria for solution in terms of the same symbolism.

Whenever these two conditions are met, we may compare symbolically generated alternatives with one another by testing them against the criteria, until we find one which is satisfactory, or the one which is the best. It is at once obvious that wherever this kind of process is possible, we do not need to "design" a solution. Indeed, we might almost claim that a problem only calls for design (in the widest sense of that word) when selection cannot be used to solve it. Whether we accept this or not, the converse anyway is true. Those problems of creating form that are traditionally called "design problems" all demand invention.

Let us see why this is so. First of all, for physical forms, we know no general symbolic way of generating new alternatives — or rather, those alternatives which we can generate by varying the existing types do not exhibit the radically new organization that solutions to new design problems demand. These can only be created by invention. Second, what is perhaps more important, we do not know how to express the criteria for success in terms of any symbolic description of a form. In other words, given a new design, there is often no mechanical way of telling, purely from the drawings which describe it, whether or not it meets its requirements. Either we must put the real thing in the actual world, and see whether it works or not, or we must use our imagination and experience of the world to predict from the drawings whether it will work or not. But there is no general symbolic connection between the requirements and the form's description which provide criteria; and so there is no way of testing the form symbolically.[3] Third, even if these first two objections could be overcome somehow, there is a much more conclusive difficulty. This is the same difficulty, precisely, that we come across in trying to construct scientific hypotheses from a given body of data. The data alone are not enough to define a hypothesis; the construction of hypotheses demands the further introduction of principles like simplicity (Occam's razor), non-arbitrariness, and clear organization.[4] The construction of form, too, requires these principles. There is at present no prospect of introducing these principles mechanically, either into science or into design. Again, they require invention.

It is therefore not possible to replace the actions of a trained designer by mechanically computed decisions. Yet at the same time the individual designer's inventive capacity is too limited for him to solve design problems successfully entirely by himself. If theory cannot be expected to invent form, how is it likely to be useful to a designer?

Let us begin by stating rather more explicitly just what part the designer does play in the process of design. I shall contrast three possible kinds of design process, schematically.

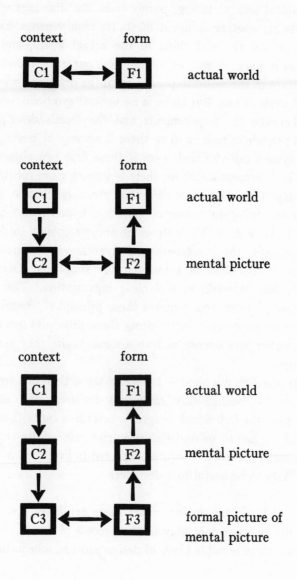

The first scheme represents the unselfconscious situation described in Chapter 4. Here the process which shapes the form is a complex two-directional interaction between the context C1 and the form F1, in the world itself. The human being is only present as an agent in this process. He reacts to misfits by changing them; but is unlikely to impose any "designed" conception on the form.

The second scheme represents the selfconscious situation described in Chapter 5. Here the design process is remote from the ensemble itself; form is shaped not by interaction between the actual context's demands and the actual inadequacies of the form, but by a conceptual interaction between the conceptual picture of the context which the designer has learned and invented, on the one hand, and ideas and diagrams and drawings which stand for forms, on the other. This interaction contains both the probing in which the designer searches the problem for its major "issues," and the development of forms which satisfy them; but its exact nature is unclear.[5] In present design practice, this critical step, during which the problem is prepared and translated into design, always depends on some kind of intuition. Though design is by nature imaginative and intuitive, and we could easily trust it if the designer's intuition were reliable, as it is it inspires very little confidence.

In the unselfconscious process there is no possibility of misconstruing the situation: nobody makes a picture of the context, so the picture cannot be wrong. But the selfconscious designer works entirely from the picture in his mind, and this picture is almost always wrong.

The way to improve this is to make a further abstract picture of our first picture of the problem, which eradicates its bias and retains only its abstract structural features; this second picture may then be examined according to precisely defined operations, in a way not subject to the bias of language and experience.[6] The third scheme in the diagram represents a third process, based on the use of such a picture. The vague and unsatisfactory picture of the context's demands, C2, which first develops in the designer's mind, is followed by this mathematical picture, C3. Similarly, but in reverse, the design F2 is preceded by an orderly complex of diagrams F3. The derivation of these diagrams F3 from C3, though still intuitive, may be clearly understood. The form is actually shaped now by a process at the third level, remote from C2 or F2. It is out in the open, and therefore under control.

This third picture, C3, is built out of mathematical entities called "sets." A set, just as its name suggests, is any collection of things whatever, without regard to common properties, and has no internal structure until it is given one.[7] A collection of riddles in a book forms a set, a lemon and an orange and an apple form a set of three fruits, a collection of relationships like fatherhood, motherhood, brotherhood, sisterhood, forms a set (in this case a set of four elements). The elements of a set can be as abstract or as concrete as you like. It must only be possible to identify them uniquely, and to distinguish them from one another.[8]

The principal ideas of set theory are these:

1. An element x of a set S, is said to belong to that set. This is written $x \in S$. A set is uniquely defined by identifying its elements.

2. One set S_1 is said to be a subset of another set S_2, if and only if every element of S_1 belongs to S_2. This

is written $S_1 \subseteq S_2$. If S_2 also contains elements which are not elements of S_1, so that S_2 is "larger" than S_1, then S_1 is called a proper subset of S_2, and we write $S_1 \subset S_2$.

3. The union of two sets S_1 and S_2 is the set of those elements which belong to either S_1 or S_2 (or both, in the case where S_1 and S_2 have elements in common). We write it as $S_1 \cup S_2$.

4. The intersection of two sets S_1 and S_2 is the set of those elements which belong to both S_1 and S_2. We write it $S_1 \cap S_2$. If S_1 and S_2 have no elements in common, this intersection is empty, and we call the sets disjoint.

Let us be specific about the use of set theory to picture design problems. We already know, from Chapter 2, what the designer's conception of a problem looks like. The problem presents itself as a task of avoiding a number of specific potential misfits between the form and some given context. Let us suppose that there are m such misfit variables: $x_1 \cdots x_m$. These misfit variables form a set. We call the set of these m misfits M, so that we may write $x_i \in M$ (for all i, $i = 1 \cdots m$).[9]

The great power and beauty of the set, as an analytical tool for design problems, is that its elements can be as various as they need be, and do not have to be restricted only to requirements which can be expressed in quantifiable form. Thus in the design of a house, the set M may contain the need for individual solitude, the need for rapid construction, the need for family comfort, the need for easy maintenance, as well as such easily quantifiable requirements as the need for low capital cost and efficiency of operation. Indeed, M may contain any requirement at all.

79

These requirements are the individual conditions which must be met at the form-context boundary, in order to prevent misfit. The field structure of this form-context boundary, in so far as the designer is aware of it, is also not hard to describe. He knows that some of the misfits interfere with one another, as he tries to solve them, or conflict; that others have common physical implications, or concur; and that still others do not interact at all. It is the presence and absence of these interactions which give the set M the system character already referred to in Chapters 3, 4, and 5.[10] We represent the interactions by associating with M a second set L, of non-directed, signed, one-dimensional elements called links, where each link joins two elements of M, and contains no other elements of M. As we shall see in Chapter 8, the links bear a negative sign if they indicate conflict, and a positive sign if they indicate concurrence, and may also be weighted to indicate strength of interaction.

The two sets M and L together define a structure known as a linear graph or topological 1-complex, which we shall refer to as $G(M,L)$, or simply G for short.[11] A typical graph is shown below. Such a graph serves as a picture of a designer's view of

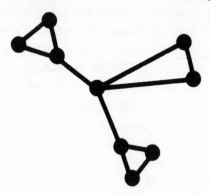

some specific problem. It is a fairly good picture, in the sense that its constituents, the sets M and L, are available to him introspectively without too much trouble; also because it keeps our attention, neatly and abstractly, on the fact that the set of misfits has a structure, or, as we called it in Chapter 2, a field.[12]

We must now explore the structure of this field. The most important and most obvious structural characteristic of any complex entity is its articulation — that is, the relative density or grouping and clustering of its component elements. We will be able to make this precise by means of the concept of a decomposition:

Informally, a decomposition of a set M into its subsidiary or subsystem sets is a hierarchical nesting of sets within sets, as is shown in the first of the two diagrams that follow. A more

usual diagram, which brings out the treelike character of the decomposition, is shown below. It refers to precisely the same structure as the other. Each element of the decomposition is a subset of those sets above it in the hierarchy.

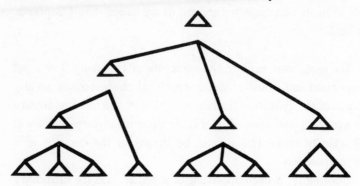

Formally I define a decomposition of a set of misfits M as a tree (or partly ordered set) of sets in which a relation of immediate subordination is defined as follows, and in which the following further conditions hold:[13]

A set S_1 is immediately subordinate to another set S_2 if and only if S_2 properly includes S_1 ($S_1 \subset S_2$), and the tree contains no further set S_3 such that $S_1 \subset S_3 \subset S_2$. Further, the tree must satisfy the following four conditions:

1. If S_i and S_j are two immediate subordinates of a set S, then $S_i \cap S_j = 0$.
2. Every set which has immediate subordinate sets is the union of all these sets.
3. There is just one set which is the immediate subordinate of no other set. This is the set M.
4. There are just m sets which have no immediate subordinates. These are the one-element sets, each of which contains one element of M.

As it stands, such a decomposition deals only with the set M. L, the set of links, plays no part in it. But it is easy to see that the existence of these links makes some of the possible decompositions very much more sensible than others. Any graph of the type $G(M,L)$ tends to pull the elements of M together in natural clusters. Our task in the next chapters is to make this precise, and to decide which decomposition of M makes the most sense, once we have a given set L associated with it. Each subset of the set M which appears in the tree will then define a subproblem of the problem M. Each subproblem will have its own integrity, and be independent of the other subproblems, so that it can be solved independently.

It is very possible, and even likely, that the way the designer initially sees the problem already hinges on a conceptual hierarchy not too much unlike a decomposition in general outline.[14] In trying to show that the links of L favor a particular decomposition, I shall really be trying to show that for every problem there is one decomposition which is especially proper to it, and that this is usually different from the one in the designer's head. For this reason we shall refer to this special decomposition as the *program* for the problem represented by $G(M,L)$. We call it a program because it provides directions or instructions to the designer, as to which subsets of M are its significant "pieces," and so which major aspects of the problem he should apply himself to. This program is a reorganization of the way the designer thinks about the problem.[15]

Finding the right design program for a given problem is the first phase of the design process. It is, if we like, the analytical phase of the process. This first phase of the process must of course be followed by the synthetic phase, in which a form is derived from the program. We shall call this synthetic phase *the realization of the program*.[1] Although these notes are given principally to the analytical phase of the process, and to the invention of programs which can make the synthesis of form a reasonable task, we must now spend a little time thinking about the way this synthesis or realization will work. Until we do so, we cannot know how to develop the details of the program.

The starting point of analysis is the requirement. The end product of analysis is a program, which is a tree of sets of requirements. The starting point of synthesis is the diagram. The end product of synthesis is the realization of the problem, which is a tree of diagrams. The program is made by decomposing a set of requirements into successively smaller subsets. The realization is made by making small diagrams and putting them together as the program directs, to get more and more complex diagrams. To achieve this we must learn to match each set of requirements in the program with a corresponding diagram.

The invention of diagrams is familiar to every designer. Any pattern which, by being abstracted from a real situation, conveys the physical influence of certain demands or forces is a diagram.

The famous stroboscopic photograph of the splash of a milk drop is, for certain purposes, a diagram of the way the forces go at the moment of impact. If you want to study these forces, this photograph, by abstracting their *immediate* physical consequences from the confusion of what you usually see when a milk drop falls, tells you a great deal about them.[2]

Le Corbusier's *ville radieuse* is a diagram, which expresses the physical consequences of two very simple basic requirements: that people should be housed at high overall density, and that they should yet all have equal and maximum access to sunlight and air.[3]

The sphere is a diagram. It expresses, among other things, the physical implications of the need to enclose as large a volume as possible within as small a surface as possible. It also expresses the implication of the requirement that a number of things be equidistant from a single point.[4]

The texture of bathers on a crowded bathing beach is a diagram. The evenness of the texture tells you that there are forces tending to place family groups as far as possible (and hence at equal distances) from one another, instead of allowing them to place themselves randomly.

An arrow is a diagram, of course, which conveys direction. Many flow problems contain requirements which can be summarized by means of arrows.[5] Very occasionally the form called for turns out to be physically arrow-shaped itself; like the case where the aerodynamic needs of a fast aeroplane are embodied in a swept-wing design.

Kekulé's representation of the benzene molecule (as atoms, with linear bonds between them) is again a diagram. Given the valency forces represented by the bonds, the diagram expresses the physical arrangement of the atoms, relative to one another, which is thought to result from the interaction of these valencies.[6]

Van Doesburg's "de Stijl" drawings, though made for other reasons, could be interpreted as diagrams which present the rectilinear consequences of the need for machine tools and rapid prefabricated assembly.[7]

The engineer's preliminary sketch for a bridge structure is a diagram. After making the initial calculations, the engineer draws some pencil lines to show himself roughly how the bridge's major members might go under the influence of gravity, the given required span, the maximum tensile strength of available steel, and so on.[8]

We notice that these diagrams may have either or both of two distinct qualities, not always equally emphasized. On the one hand they may summarize aspects of a physical structure, by presenting one of the constituent patterns of its organization (as the photograph of the milk splash does, or the drawings for the *ville radieuse*). Although we can often infer a great deal about the demands responsible for the particular pattern such a diagram exhibits, it remains principally a description of formal characteristics. We shall call such a diagram a form diagram. On the other hand, the diagram may be intended to summarize a set of functional properties or constraints, like the arrow, or the population density map. This kind of diagram is principally a notation for the problem, rather than for the form. We shall call such a diagram a requirement diagram.

Let us consider extreme examples of a requirement diagram and a form diagram for a simple object. The mathematical statement $F = kv^2$ expresses the fact that under certain conditions the energy lost by a moving object because of friction depends on the square of its velocity. In the design of a racing car, it is obviously important to reduce this effect as far as possible; and in this sense the mathematical statement is a requirement diagram. At the other extreme, a watercolor perspective view of a racing car is also a diagram. It summarizes certain physical aspects of the car's organization, and is therefore a legitimate form diagram. Yet clearly neither the equation nor the water color is very useful as such, in the search for form. To be useful, the equation needs to be interpreted, so that one can understand its physical consequences. Similarly the drawing needs to be drawn in such a way that the functional consequences of the car's shape are clearly comprehensible. Let us put this another way. A requirement diagram becomes useful only if it contains physical implications, that is, if it has the elements of a form diagram in it. A form diagram becomes useful only if its functional consequences are foreseeable, that is, if it has the elements of a requirement diagram in it. A diagram which expresses requirements alone or form alone is no help in effecting the translation of requirements into form, and will not play any constructive part in the search for form. We shall call a diagram constructive if and only if it is both at once — if and only if it is a requirement diagram and a form diagram at the same time. Let us consider an example.

Suppose that two streets of an existing town center are to be widened at and around their point of intersection, to lessen congestion. Suppose further that the only requirement is that today's traffic can flow without congestion. The requirement diagram, therefore, consists basically of information about how much traffic flows in various directions at different times of day. It is possible to present this information in a nonconstructive diagram by simply tabulating the flow numerically for each of the twelve possible paths, for different times of day. It is also possible, however, to present this same information in the condensed graphic form shown below.

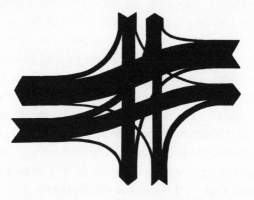

Here we have a street map with arrows of various widths on it, representing the number of vehicles per hour flowing in various directions at peak hours. In this form the diagram indicates directly what form the new intersection must take. Clearly a thick arrow requires a wide street, so that the overall pattern called for emerges directly from the diagram.[9] It is both a requirement diagram and a form diagram. This diagram is a constructive one.

The constructive diagram is the bridge between requirements and form. But its great beauty is that it goes deeper still. The same duality between requirement and form which the constructive diagram is able to express and unify also appears at a second level: the duality is itself characteristic of our knowledge of form.

Every form can be described in two ways: from the point of view of what it is, and from the point of view of what it does. What it is is sometimes called the formal description. What it does, when it is put in contact with other things, is sometimes called the functional description.

Here are some formal descriptions. A raincoat is three feet long, made of polythene $\frac{1}{2}$ mm thick, its sleeves cut in such and such a way, and so on. A salt crystal is a cubical arrangement of alternating sodium and chloride ions. A human body contains a heart, of such and such a size, in this position in the chest, a pair of kidneys rather lower and further back, and so on again. These descriptions specify size, position, pattern, material.

The corresponding functional descriptions tell you what happens when these objects are put in various contexts in the world. The raincoat is impervious to rain, and melts when heated. The salt crystal is transparent, conducts electricity slightly, dissolves in water but not in oil, shatters when hit hard with a hammer, and so on. The heart beats faster at high altitudes, the kidneys work when the body is fed.

In many of these cases we should find it hard to relate the two descriptions to one another, because we do not understand the objects thoroughly enough, and do not know, say, how the arrangement of atoms in a crystal relates to the solubility of the crystal in different solutes. However, for some very simple objects, there is virtually no rift between formal and functional descriptions. Take a soap bubble for instance, or a soap film on a wire frame. The behavior of soap films is so thoroughly understood that we know the functional properties of any given physical arrangement, and we know what shapes and sizes of bubbles different external conditions lead to.[10] In this case, the formal descriptions and the functional descriptions are just different ways of saying the same things; we can say, if we like, that we have a unified description of a soap bubble. This unified description is the abstract equivalent of a constructive diagram.

It is the aim of science to give such a unified description for every object and phenomenon we know. The task of chemistry (and it has been remarkably successful in this) is to relate functional and formal descriptions of chemical compounds to one another, so that we can go backwards and forwards between the two, without loss in understanding. The task of physiology has been to relate the functional behavior of the body to the organs we observe in anatomy. Again, it has been reasonably successful.

The solution of a design problem is really only another effort to find a unified description. The search for realization through constructive diagrams is an effort to understand the required form so fully that there is no longer a rift between its functional specification and the shape it takes.[11]

In other words, a constructive diagram, if it is a good one, actually contributes to our understanding of the functional specification which calls it into being.

We have already seen, in Chapter 2, that the designer never really understands the context fully. He may know, piecemeal, what the context demands of the form. But he does not see the context as a single pattern — a unitary field of forces. If he is a good designer the form he invents will penetrate the problem so deeply that it not only solves it but illuminates it.

A well-designed house not only fits its context well but also illuminates the problem of just what the context is, and thereby clarifies the life which it accommodates. Thus Le Corbusier's invention of new house forms in the 1920's really represented part of the modern attempt to understand the twentieth century's new way of life.[12]

The airfoil wing section which allows airplanes to fly was invented at a time when it had just been "proved" that no machine heavier than air could fly. Its aerodynamic properties were not understood until some time after it had been in use. Indeed the invention and use of the airfoil made a substantial contribution to the development of aerodynamic theory, rather than vice versa.[13]

At the time of its invention the geodesic dome could not be calculated on the basis of the structural calculations then in use. Its invention not only solved a specific problem, but drew attention to a different way of thinking about load-bearing structures.[14]

In all these cases, the invention is based on a hunch which actually makes it easier to understand the problem. Like such a hunch, a constructive diagram will often precede the precise knowledge which could prescribe its shape on rational grounds.

It is therefore quite reasonable to think of the realization as a way of probing the context's nature, beyond the program but parallel to it. This is borne out, perhaps, by the recent tendency among designers to think of their designs as hypotheses.[15] Each constructive diagram is a tentative assumption about the nature of the context. Like a hypothesis, it relates an unclear set of forces to one another conceptually; like a hypothesis, it is usually improved by clarity and economy of notation.[16] Like a hypothesis, it cannot be obtained by deductive methods, but only by abstraction and invention. Like a hypothesis, it is rejected when a discrepancy turns up and shows that it fails to account for some new force in the context.

The constructive diagram can describe the context, and it can describe the form. It offers us a way of probing the context, and a way of searching for form. Because it manages to do both simultaneously, it offers us a bridge between requirements and form, and therefore is a most important tool in the process of design.

In all design tasks the designer has to translate sets of requirements into diagrams which capture their physical implications. In a literal sense these diagrams are no more than stages on the way to the specification of a form, like the circulation diagram of a building, or the expected population density map for some region under development. They specify only gross pattern aspects of the form. But the path from these diagrams to the final design is a matter of local detail. The form's basic organization is born precisely in the constructive diagrams which precede its design.

What we must now see is that the constructive diagram is not only useful in probing the more obvious, known aspects of a problem like circulation, but that it can also be used to create the newly discovered implications of a new problem. We have seen that the *extension* of any problem may be captured by a set of requirements; and that by the same token any new set of requirements may be regarded as the definition of a new problem. Going one step further, the *intension* (or physical meaning) of a known problem may be captured by a diagram; and by the same token the intension of any new, hitherto unconnected, set of requirements may be captured by a new diagram.[17]

The problem is defined by a set of requirements called M. The solution to this problem will be a form which successfully satisfies all of these requirements. This form could be developed, in all its important details, as a single constructive diagram for the set M, if it were not for the complexity of M's internal interactions (represented by L), which makes it impossible to find such a diagram directly. Can we find it indirectly? Are there some simpler diagrams which the designer *can* construct, and which will contribute substantially to his ability to find a diagram for M? There are; and the program tells us how to find them.

The program is a hierarchy of the most significant subsets of M. Each subset is a subproblem with its own integrity. In the program the smallest sets fall together in larger sets; and these in turn again in larger sets. Each subset can be translated into a constructive diagram. And each of these subsets of M, because it contains fewer requirements than M itself, and less interaction between them, is simpler to diagram than M. It is therefore natural to begin by constructing diagrams for the smallest sets prescribed by the program. If we build up compound diagrams from these simplest diagrams according to the program's structure, and build up further compound diagrams from these in turn, we get a tree of diagrams. This tree of diagrams contains just one diagram for each set of requirements in the program's tree. We call it the realization of the program.

It is easy to bring out the contrast between the analytical nature of the program and the synthetic nature of its realiza-

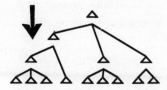 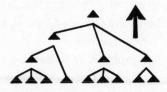

Program, consisting of sets   Realization, consisting of diagrams

tion. As we see on the left, the tree of sets is obtained by successive division and partition. The tree of diagrams, on the right, is made by successive composition and fusion. At its apex is the last diagram, which captures the full implications of the whole problem, and is therefore the complete diagram for the form required. Examples of these two trees are given in Appendix 1.

We have seen roughly now how we shall try to represent a design problem by means of a graph, $G(M,L)$; that we shall then decompose the set M to give us a program; and how this program will be used as a basis for the construction of diagrams from which we can develop a form. We now come to the precise details of the analysis that defines the program. We begin, in this chapter, by establishing the exact character of the sets M and L which together provide us with the graph $G(M,L)$.

The problem presents itself, originally, when the ensemble is given, and when the proposed boundary between context and form, within that ensemble, is chosen. At this stage the problem is only defined within rather broad limits. Typical examples are these. We are to design a highway system for New York City; a kettle for use in the technical and cultural environment provided by metropolitan U.S.A. of 1965; a new town, for 30,000 people, forty miles from London. The context, in these cases, is fixed, and will remain constant for the duration of the problem; it may therefore be described in as much detail as possible. On the other hand, the nature of the required form is uncertain. It may be given a name, perhaps, like "kettle" or "town," to make the problem specific; but one of the designer's first tasks will be to strip the problem of the preconceptions which such names introduce.

Now, as we know already, the set M consists of all those possible kinds of misfit which might occur between the form and the context; in the case of the kettle–metropolitan U.S.A. ensemble, this set includes specific economic limitations, technical requirements of production, functional performance standards, matters of safety and appearance, and so on.[1] To be exact, each element of M is a variable which can be in one of two states: fit and misfit.[2] It is important to remember that the state of this variable depends on the entire ensemble. We cannot decide whether a misfit has occurred either by looking at the form alone, or by looking at the context alone. Misfit is a condition of the ensemble as a whole, which comes from the unsatisfactory interaction of the form and context.

Take capital cost. The variable's two states are "too expensive," which represents misfit, and "OK," which represents fit. If a kettle is too expensive, this describes a property of the kettle plus its context — that is, of the ensemble. Out of context, the kettle's price either exceeds or does not exceed various figures we can name: nothing more. Only its relation to the rest of the ensemble makes it "too expensive" or "all right." In other words, it depends on how much we can afford. Again, take the kettle's capacity. If we look at the kettle by itself, all we can say is that it holds such and such a quantity of water. We cannot say whether this is enough, until we see what the context demands. Again, the fact that the kettle does not hold enough water, or that it does, is a property of the form plus context taken as a whole. This fact, that the variable describes the ensemble as a whole, and never the form alone, leads to the following important principle. In principle, to decide whether or not a form meets a given requirement, we must construct it, put it in contact with the context in question, and test the ensemble so formed to see whether misfit occurs in it or not. You can only tell whether a kettle is comfortable enough to hold by picking it up. In principle, you can only decide whether a road is wide enough to drive down by constructing it, and trying to drive a car down it under the conditions it is supposed to meet.

Of course we do not stick to this principle in practice; it would be impossibly inconvenient if we had to. If we know the maximum width of cars to be used on the highway, and also know that for comfortable driving and adequate room for braking at a certain speed you need an extra 2'6" on either side, we can tell in advance whether or not a given roadway is going to cause this kind of misfit or not. We can do so because the measurable character of the property "width" allows us to establish a connection between the width of the roadway and the likelihood of malfunction in the ensemble. What we do in such a case, to simplify the design task, is to establish a performance standard — in this case specifying that all roadways must have a minimum lane width of 11'0" perhaps, because large cars are 6' wide. We can then say, with a reasonable amount of confidence, that every road which meets this standard will not cause this misfit in the ensemble.

We can set up such a performance standard for every misfit variable that exhibits continuous variation along a well-defined scale. Other typical examples are acoustic separation of rooms (noise reduction can be expressed in decibels), illumination for comfortable reading (expressed in lumens per sq. ft.), load-bearing capacity required to prevent danger of structural failure (safety factor times maximum expected load), reasonable maintenance costs (expressed in dollars per year). Once a scale like this has been found for a requirement, it is then almost always possible to find a connection between this scale and some intrinsic property of the form;[3] thus, given a house design on the drawing board, it is possible to calculate probable maintenance costs, the noise reduction between rooms, and so on; it is then, of course, no longer necessary to find out by trial and error whether the form fails to fit its context in these respects. A performance standard determined by the context can be decided for each of them in advance, and used as a criterion of fit. For this reason there is a growing tendency to look for suitable scales, and to set up performance standards, for as many requirements as possible.[4]

However, the existence of a performance standard, and the association of a numerical scale with a misfit variable, does not mean that the misfit is any more keenly felt in the ensemble when it occurs. There are of course many, many misfits for which we do not have such a scale. Some typical examples are "boredom in an exhibition," "comfort for a kettle handle," "security for a fastener or a lock," "human warmth in a living room," "lack of variety in a park." No one has yet invented a scale for unhappiness or discomfort or uneasiness, and it is therefore not possible to set up performance standards for them. Yet these misfits are among the most critical which occur in design problems.

The importance of these nonquantifiable variables is sometimes lost in the effort to be "scientific." A variable which exhibits continuous variation is easier to manipulate mathematically, and therefore seems more suitable for a scientific treatment. But although it is certainly true that the use of performance standards makes it less necessary for a designer to rely on personal experience, it also happens that the kind of mathematical optimization which quantifiable variables make possible is largely irrelevant to the design problem.

A design problem is not an optimization problem.[5] In other words, it is not a problem of meeting any one requirement or any function of a number of requirements in the *best possible* way (though we may sometimes speak loosely as though it were, and may actually try to optimize one or two things like cost or construction time). For most requirements it is important only to satisfy them at a level which suffices to prevent misfit between the form and the context, and to do this in the least arbitrary manner possible.[6] This is a strictly binary situation. The task is to bring each binary variable to the value 0 (for continuous variables the value 0 corresponds to the whole range of values on the "good" side of the required performance standard). It is therefore only important that each variable be specific enough and clearly enough defined, so that any actual design can be classified unambiguously as a fit or misfit.

For quantifiable variables this is easy. An obvious example, in the case of the kettle, is the need for adequate capacity. Since the capacity of a kettle can be described quantitatively, we can therefore very easily set up a standard capacity which we require of satisfactory kettles, and call smaller capacity a misfit for kettles. Then we say that this variable takes the value 0 for kettles with a capacity greater than or equal to the critical capacity, and the value 1 for kettles with smaller capacity. The natural scale of capacity measurement provides an objective basis for dividing kettles into those which fit the context in this respect, and those which don't.

For nonquantifiable variables, it is not quite so easy. Take the property "comfortable to hold" for kettles. There is no objectively measurable property that is known to correlate well enough with comfort to serve as a scale of "comfortableness." However, such a misfit variable can still be well enough defined. We can set up communicable limits which a group of experts can understand well enough to agree about classifying designs. We can certainly explain what we mean by comfort clearly enough, in commonsense language, for a group of people to learn to agree about which kettles are comfortable to hold, and which are not. This makes comfortableness an acceptable variable, for the purpose of the present analysis.

We shall treat a property of the ensemble (quantifiable or not), as an acceptable misfit variable, provided we can associate with it an unambiguous way of dividing all possible forms into two classes: those for which we agree that they fit or meet the requirement, which we describe by saying that the variable takes the value 0, and those for which we do not agree, which therefore fail to meet the requirement, and for which the variable is assigned the value 1.

This brings us to three questions, which may seem hard to answer.

1. How can we get an exhaustive set of variables M for a given problem; in other words, how can we be sure we haven't left out some important issue?
2. How do we know that all the variables we include in the list M are relevant to the problem?
3. For any specific variable, how do we decide at what point misfit occurs; or if it is a continuous variable, how do we know what value to set as a performance

standard? In other words, how do we recognize the condition so far described as misfit?

These questions have already been answered, substantially, in Chapter 2. Let us remind ourselves of the fundamental principle. *Any state of affairs in the ensemble which derives from the interaction between form and context, and causes stress in the ensemble, is a misfit.*

This concept of stress or misfit is a primitive one. We shall proceed without defining it. We may find precedents for this in the practice of common law, psychiatry, medicine, engineering, anthropology, where it also serves as a primitive undefined concept.[7] In all these cases, stress is said to occur wherever it can be shown, in a common-sense way, that some state of affairs is somehow detrimental to the unity and well-being of the whole ensemble. In design too, though it may seem hard to define the concept of stress in theory, it is easy in practice. In architecture, for example, when the context is defined by a client, this client will tell you in no uncertain terms what he won't put up with. Again, it is obvious that a kettle which is uncomfortable to hold causes stress, since the context demands that it should be comfortable to hold. The fact that the kettle is for use by human hands makes this no more than common sense. At the opposite extreme, if somebody suggests that the ensemble is stressed if the kettle will not reflect ultraviolet radiation, common sense tells us to reject this — unless some special reason can be given, which shows what damage the absorption of ultraviolet does to the ensemble.

This principle that stress or misfit is a primitive concept has the following consequences. First of all, it is clearly not possible to list all the types of stress which might occur in an ensemble exhaustively, and therefore impossible to hope that M could provide an exhaustive description of a problem. A moment's thought will convince us that we are never capable of stating a design problem except in terms of the errors we have observed in past solutions to past problems. Even if we try to design something for an entirely new purpose that has never been conceived before, the best we can do in stating the problem is to anticipate how it might possibly go wrong by scanning mentally all the ways in which other things have gone wrong in the past.

The best we can do therefore is to include in M all those kinds of stress which we can imagine. The set M can never be properly called complete. The process of design, even when it has become selfconscious, remains a process of error-reduction, and the set M remains a temporary catalogue of those errors which seem to need correction.

The fact that the design process must be viewed as an error-correcting process has a further consequence. The errors that seem most critical to one person will not be the same as those which seem most critical to another. Any list of errors or misfits, which are to be removed, therefore necessarily has something of a personal flavor.

For a problem like an urban dwelling, if we ask different designers to state the problem, we may find it hard even to get agreement about what the relevant issues are. Probably each designer has his private set of hunches about "where the issue really lies." The designer is free to look at a problem in any way he chooses; all we can hope to do is to put a fruitful structure on his view of it. It is for this reason that M cannot be thought of as objectively complete, and has been presented, instead, in Chapter 6, as a picture of a designer's view of a problem.

However, it should be pointed out that in spite of the natural bias which any one designer's statement of a problem is sure to carry, at the same time the use of the set M as a means of representation does have in it one great claim to neutrality. What designers disagree about is the relative importance of different requirements. In the present theory this would have to be expressed, if it were expressed at all, by assigning some sorts of weights or values to different variables. However, few designers will actually disagree about the variables themselves. While the relative importance of different requirements usually is a matter of personal opinion, the decision that a requirement either is a requirement or isn't, is less personal. The stress a misfit causes, whether slight or not, has simple tangible consequences which can be objectively determined. By leaving the designer to work out the relative importance of different requirements at his own discretion during the diagram phase of the design process, it is therefore possible for designers to agree about the contents of the set M, whether or not they agree about their relative importance, because mere inclusion of a requirement in M, as such, attaches no weight to it.

Before we say any more about the precise logical properties the misfit variables must have, we shall now define the interaction between variables. In order to do this, we must introduce a new concept: the domain of forms for which these variables are defined. Let us call it D. This domain D may be thought of roughly as the set of all those discriminable forms (good and bad) which might possibly be placed in contact with the given context to complete the ensemble. The contents of this domain cannot be specified precisely (if they could, the design problem would become a selection problem); the domain is imaginary, but serves to anchor the idea of inter-variable connections. We should think of it as the totality of possible forms within the cognitive reach of the designer. In other words, it is a shorthand way of talking about all those discriminable forms which a designer can imagine and design.[8]

Now, we know by postulate, that we can in principle decide, for each one of the forms in D, which requirements it meets, and which it fails to meet. This means that each misfit variable x_i cuts the domain D in two: into a set of those forms which fit, and a set of those which don't. Schematically we show this:

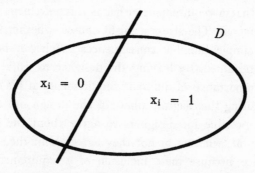

From two variables we get four sets, in which the forms take values as shown below.

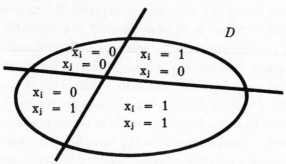

If we superimpose all m variables, we get a division of the domain D into 2^m mutually exclusive classes, each labeled by a different pattern of values for $x_1 \cdots x_m$. We shall call the proportion of forms in D which do not satisfy requirement x_i the probability of the misfit x_i occurring. We write this $p(x_i = 1)$. (Naturally $0 \leqslant p(x_i = 1) \leqslant 1$.) In the same way we define the probability of avoiding the misfit x_i as $p(x_i = 0)$; and the probability of avoiding both x_i and x_j simultaneously as $p(x_i = 0, x_j = 0)$, and so forth.

If the variables $x_1 \cdots x_m$ are all pairwise independent then it is an axiom of probability theory that we may write $p(x_i = 0, x_j = 0) = p(x_i = 0) \cdot p(x_j = 0)$ for all i and j. And similarly if the variables are also three-way, four-way and n-way independent, then these independence relations hold for the conditional probabilities, and we write, for example, $p(x_i = 0, x_j = 0 \mid x_k = 1) = p(x_i = 0 \mid x_k = 1) \cdot p(x_j = 0 \mid x_k = 1)$ conditional on $x_k = 1$ and so on.[9]

Wherever the variables are not independent, the above relations break down. Essentially, then, we speak of a dependence among two variables wherever $p(x_i = 0, x_j = 0)$ is markedly unequal to $p(x_i = 0) \cdot p(x_j = 0)$, and similarly for more than two variables. Formally, we describe these dependences by means of the correlation coefficients.[10] The simplest correlation coefficient is that for two variables: [11]

$$c_{ij} = \frac{p(x_i=0,x_j=0) \cdot p(x_i=1,x_j=1) - p(x_i=0,x_j=1) \cdot p(x_i=1,x_j=0)}{[p(x_i=0)p(x_j=0)p(x_i=1)p(x_j=1)]^{\frac{1}{2}}}.$$

For any pair of variables x_i and x_j, then, we may distinguish the following three possibilities.

1. If c_{ij} is markedly less than 0, x_i and x_j conflict; like "The kettle's being too small" and "The kettle's oc-

cupying too much space." When we look for a form which avoids x_1 we weaken our chances of avoiding the other, x_2.

2. If c_{ij} is markedly greater than 0, x_i and x_j concur; like "the kettle's not being able to withstand the temperature of boiling water" and "the kettle's being liable to corrode in steamy kitchens." When we look for materials which avoid one of these difficulties, we improve our chances of avoiding the other.

3. If c_{ij} is not far from 0, x_i and x_j exhibit no noticeable interaction of either type.

In the first case we should write a negative link between the variables, in the second case we should write a positive link between them, and in the third case we should write no link at all between them. Roughly speaking, two requirements interact (and are therefore linked), if what you do about one of them in a design necessarily makes it more difficult or easier to do anything about the other.[12]

This at once suggests a simple way of estimating links, based on direct inspection of the known existing forms. Suppose we pick a sample of all the recently produced kettles we can find and examine it from the point of view of misfits x_i and x_j. Since we have defined each misfit variable in such a way that we can always decide which value it takes (0 or 1) in a given design, the proportions of kettles in our sample where x_i only has occurred ($x_i = 1, x_j = 0$), where x_j only has occurred ($x_i = 0, x_j = 1$), where both have occurred ($x_i = 1, x_j = 1$), and where neither has occurred ($x_i = 0, x_j = 0$), are easy to obtain. Provided the samples are carefully chosen, these sample proportions give us good estimates of the probability of x_i, of x_j, of both, of neither, occurring in a randomly selected contemporary kettle. From these joint two-variable probability estimates, we could compute the correlation c_{ij}, and write a link between any pair of variables whose correlation was statistically significant. We could use the same procedure to decide on the many-variable correlations.

However, such a method, being based on a sample of existing kettles, is not what we want at all. If we think carefully, we see that empirically found correlations have very different degrees of validity. Some are almost logically necessary — like the conflict between the need for sufficient capacity in the kettle and the need for economical storage space. The first calls for large volume, the second for small volume. This conflict exists almost by definition, at least until one is thinking of ways of heating water that are very much unlike kettles.[13]

Other correlations depend on physical laws — like the conflict between the need for a material which keeps the heat in after the kettle has boiled and the need for a material which allows the kettle water to be heated cheaply. It is hard to imagine a material whose thermal conductivity is different in opposite directions; so again, although there are ways round it, the conflict exists for most of the kettles one can imagine.

But other correlations will depend only on accidents of present taste and habit. If you look at kettles in the shops today, you might notice that the cheap ones have tin handles, and you might conclude that the need for safety when you pick up a hot kettle (that is, for a handle which doesn't burn you) conflicts with the economics of production and the need to keep down capital cost. However, this conclusion, being based on a sample of presently available kettles, will change as soon as we begin to think of other materials and designs. This conflict certainly does not exist for all imaginable kettles.

Clearly we want to avoid muddling this last kind of case with the other two. If we were to accept the linkage it suggests, then together with the essential logic of the ensemble we should also be freezing in its most temporary incidentals. We are interested in those links between variables which hold for all forms we can conceive (that is, for the whole of D). Any sample based on those possible solutions which happen to have been constructed is heavily biased toward the past. To avoid the bias we should need either to examine all the members of D exhaustively or to find a theory which offers us a way of sampling D unbiasedly. Neither of these is practicable today.

However, we may overcome the bias by another means. Instead of just looking for statistical connections between variables, we may try to find causal relations between them. Blind belief based only on observed regularity is not very strong, because it is not the result of a seen causal connection. But if we can invent an explanation for inter-variable correlation in terms of some conceptual model, we shall be much better inclined to believe in the regularity, because we shall then know which kinds of extraneous circumstances are likely to upset the regularity and which are not. We call a correlation "causal" in this second case, when we have some kind of understanding or model whose rules account for it.

For example, the molecular and crystalline structure of materials gives us good reason to believe that the thermal conductivity of a material is the same in any two opposite directions, and hence that the need to heat a kettle quickly conflicts with the need to keep the water hot once it has boiled. In this case, because we "understand" the connection between the two variables, we call it causal, and give it much greater weight — because we are convinced that it holds for almost all conceivable possibilities.

The search for causal relations of this sort cannot be mechanically experimental or statistical; it requires interpretation: to practice it we must adopt the same kind of common sense that we have to make use of all the time in the inductive part of science. The data of scientific method never go further than to display regularities. We put structure into them only by inference and interpretation.[14] In just the same way, the structural facts about a system of variables in an ensemble will come only from the thoughtful interpretation of observations.

We shall say that two variables interact if and only if the designer can find some reason (or conceptual model) which makes sense to him and tells him why they should do so.[15]

Again, as with the definition of the variables, this introduces a personal bias, and reminds us that L, like M, is a picture of the way the designer sees the problem, not an objective description of the problem itself. If the designer sees a conflict between the need to have sufficient capacity in a kettle and the need to conserve storage space, he does so because he has certain preconceptions in mind about the kinds of kettle which are possible. It is true that there are conceivable devices, not yet invented, for boiling water as it comes out of the faucet, and that these might take very little storage space. But until the designer understands this possibility, there is no point in telling him that the conflict is spurious; as far as he is concerned, there really is a conflict, which needs to be resolved, and therefore needs to be included in L and taken into account in the analysis of M. It is only after first including this link in L, and in the very act of asking himself whether two variables really do interact, and why they do, that the designer sees the possibility of avoiding the conflict and so sees further into the problem.

The reader may well ask how such a process, in which both the requirements and the links between requirements are defined by the designer from things already present in his mind, can possibly have any outcome which is not also already present in the designer's mind. In other words, how can all this process really be helpful? The answer is that, because it concentrates on structure, the process is able to make a coherent and therefore new whole out of incoherent pieces.

It is true that the designer must already have some physical ideas about the problem in his mind when he starts. In order to define requirements, he must be aware of the specific physical implications of each. In order to define links between requirements, he must be aware of the many specific ways in which these physical implications are likely to conflict and to concur. But the many piecemeal implications which the designer is aware of do not themselves amount to form. He is only able to define form at that moment when these physical implications coalesce in his mind, and take on organized shape. The process I am describing, as we shall see, helps precisely here, by forcing *organization* onto the specific but hitherto unorganized details in the designer's mind.

Undoubtedly the pattern of interactions in any real-world problem will have a great variety of different strengths. In one case two variables may conflict so strongly that they virtually exclude one another and can never take the same values at the same time. In another case, there may be no more than a barely discernible tendency for them to concur. But while an explicitly statistical test would give the interactions a continuous range of values, the *ad hoc* methods of practical common sense will hardly allow us to assign them a consistently scaled continuous range — particularly in view of the fact that different consultants may have incommensurable personal scales of evaluation, and that interactions which spring from different kinds of sources can be hard to compare. In practice we shall, at best, be able to distinguish two or three strengths of interaction.

In practice, then, we shall give each pair of variables (x_i, x_j) some small integral index, ν_{ij}, equal to 0 if there is no interaction, positive if there is concurrence, negative for conflict. It will usually be convenient to keep the absolute value of ν_{ij} less than or equal to some fixed integer ν. For the sake of consistent interpretation, assume that the link index ν_{ij} indicates a correlation of $\delta \nu_{ij}$, where δ is some arbitrary constant, such that $\delta \nu \leqslant 1$. We may display the values of the ν_{ij} in matrix form. The cell in the ith row and the jth column contains the value ν_{ij}. Thus the cell in the 1st row and the 2nd column $(i = 1, j = 2)$ contains ν_{12}. The matrix is symmetrical. Thus

	x_1	x_2	x_3
x_1	0	2	0
x_2	2	0	-1
x_3	0	-1	0

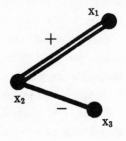

III

From this matrix we define the set L as a set of links associated with the variables of M, as follows.[16] For every pair of variables x_i and x_j, there are $|\nu_{ij}|$ distinct elements of L which join x_i to x_j. These elements bear the same sign as the index ν_{ij}, negative for conflict, and positive for concurrence.[17] The sets M and L together, completely define the graph $G(M,L)$.[18]

The definitions we have given so far still leave certain practical questions about the sets M and L unanswered. Does it matter, for instance, if two variables are very close in meaning, though slightly different? How specific or how general must they be? What do we do about three-variable interaction? The answers to these questions depend on three important formal properties of the system $G(M,L)$, which we shall now explore.

First of all, if the graph $G(M,L)$ is to give us an accurate picture of the variables' behavior, it is necessary that the set L describe *all* the interaction between variables which there is. Since the elements of L are links which represent two-variable correlation, this means that the variables must be chosen to be free from three-variable and higher-order correlations. The mathematics of Appendix 2 is also based on the assumption that the higher-order correlations vanish.[19] If this is not so, any analysis based on M and L alone is sure to give misleading results.

Second, even the two-variable correlation $\delta\nu_{ij}$ must be small, for each pair of variables. Specifically, as far as the mathematics of Appendix 2 is concerned, we must have $l\delta \leqslant 1$, where l is the total number of links in L.[20]

Third, the analysis in Appendix 2 is also based on the assumption of a certain simple symmetry among the variables of M. It demands that $p(x_i = 0)$ should be the same for all i.[21] Again, if this is not so, the analysis will be invalid.

Let us now consider the practical implications of these three formal properties which the system $G(M,L)$ must have. We take the last one first. It demands that $p(x_i = 0)$ should be the same for all i, or that the proportion of all thinkable forms which satisfy a requirement should be about the same for each requirement. What this amounts to, in common-sense language, is that all the variables should be roughly comparable in their scope and significance.

We cannot admit "economically satisfactory" as one requirement, and "maintenance costs low enough" as another. Plainly these have different degrees of significance, because the second is part of the first, while the first is not part of the second. Every design which is economically satisfactory must *a fortiori* have acceptable maintenance costs. But the reverse is not true. There are far more possible designs which meet the second than the first, because the first is much wider in scope and significance; their probabilities of occurrence are very unequal. In this case the inequality is especially clear because the second requirement is, as it were, contained in the first. But the difference would be just as great if we replaced the first by "functionally satisfactory." This is again wider in scope and significance than "maintenance costs low enough" even though it does not contain it. If we want to use "maintenance costs low enough" as one requirement, then we must break down "functionally satisfactory" into smaller, more specific requirements, comparable to it. The first step in constructing the set M is to make all its variables approximately equal in "size" or scope.[22]

Let us take the second of the three formal properties next.

In practice, of course, the preciseness of this mathematical expression is meaningless, since we judge the correlations "by eye," and do not obtain them numerically. What it does mean, in practice, though, is that we must be satisfied that all the variables are as independent as we can get them to be. An example should make this clear: Suppose the following two variables appear on our list, for the kettle problem.

1. "The kettle must heat water fast enough."
2. "The kettle must keep water hot once it is heated."

These two are clearly not at all independent. However, there are two fairly independent issues lurking behind them, if we can only find them. One way to bring this out would be by the following rearrangement, which covers more or less the same ground as the first pair, but consists of two more independent variables.

3. "The kettle must permit one-way heat transmission only."
4. "The kettle must have low thermal capacity."

A considerable amount of energy must be spent in the preliminary stages shuffling and reshuffling the variables in this fashion, until they are as independent as they can be made.[23]

The first formal property, that the three-variable or higher-order correlations among the elements of M should be negligible, is the hardest of all to achieve. It means that the two-variable correlation for any pair of variables must be independent of the states of all other variables. Since the state of one variable is most likely to affect the correlation between other variables, if that one variable is wide in scope the best we can do in satisfying this is to make all the individual variables as specific and minute as possible.

This policy of making all the variables highly specific is important for another reason. However much we may try to steer clear of existing categories, in practice we shall always have to generate the specific variables of M through intermediate stages. The brain is not made to think of such detailed lists amorphously. Whether we like it or not, if we think of one variable which has to do with acoustics, we shall inevitably then think of others which seem, to us, to fall under the same heading or to be in the same conceptual area. It is therefore a matter of practical psychology that we cannot avoid using superordinate concepts like "economics" and "acoustics" altogether, as intermediate steps in the task of listing misfit variables. At best we may treat these conceptual intermediates as key words, as loosely conceived labels for the principal issues in the problem, which we shall then break down further into finer pieces to get our set of variables M. The closer our variables are to these abstract and general key words, the more susceptible the problem remains to the kind of distortions discussed in Chapter 5. The more specific and detailed we make the variables, the less constrained $G(M,L)$ will be by previous conceptions, and the more open to detailed and unbiased examination of its causal structure.

Let us therefore sum up the properties the elements of M must have. They must be chosen (1) to be of equal scope, (2) to be as independent of one another as is reasonably possible, and (3) to be as small in scope and hence as specific and detailed and numerous as possible.[24] An example of a set M is given in Appendix 1, together with its associated set L.

We now have a graph $G(M,L)$ which represents the design problem. As we have seen in Chapter 6, to solve the problem, we shall try to decompose the set M in such a way that it gives us a helpful program for design. We shall now consider what criterion to use as a basis for decomposition.

As we observed in Chapter 6, a program really gives us a series of simpler subproblems, and tells us in what order to solve them. Before we try to define a decomposition criterion we may want to question the assumption that such a decomposition can be of any use at all to a designer. The designer as a form-maker is looking for integrity (in the sense of singleness); he wishes to form a unit, to synthesize, to bring elements together. A design program's origin, on the other hand, is analytical, and its effect is to fragment the problem. The opposition between these two aims, analysis and synthesis, has sometimes led people to maintain that in design intellect and art are incompatible, and that no analytical process can help a designer form unified well-organized designs.

Let us look at this objection to analysis more closely. It is a common experience that attempts to solve one piece of a problem first, then others, and so on, lead to endless involutions. You no sooner solve one aspect of a thing than another is put out of joint. And when you go back to correct that one, something else goes wrong. You go round and round in circles, unable ever to produce a form which is thoroughly right, because there is no way of integrating the pieces you have tackled independently. This is the great argument against attempts to solve design problems piecemeal. And it is argued further that, since no amount of analyzable juggling can ever solve this difficulty, the designer has to rely on a subconscious creative force to juggle the pieces more successfully. His hand and eye must be secure enough, in other words, to take him to his answer more immediately than his intelligence can. If design problems were homogeneous, this recommendation would be important. For then any analytical subdivision would, so to speak, put cracks in them, which would destroy their unity. As it happens though, in practice problems are not homogeneous. They are full of knots and crevices which exhibit a well-defined structure. An analytical process fails only if it does not take this structure into account. If we can learn to draw the gross structural components of the problem out of the graph $G(M,L)$ which represents it, the difficulty will disappear.

The question is, how are these separable structural components of a problem to be recognized? We face this kind of task every day, constantly, even when we see nothing more complicated than a pair of oranges on a table side by side. In seeing two oranges lying side by side, and not one and a half oranges lying next to half an orange, we have recognized the structural components correctly. (Correctly, of course, because while we can pick either orange up and leave the other where it is, we cannot pick up $1\frac{1}{2}$ oranges, and leave $\frac{1}{2}$ an orange lying there.) Köhler and Wertheimer drew attention to the fact that even an apparently simple cognitive act like

this, in fact demands a very complex perceptual operation.[1]
It is not surprising to find, in the similar but more abstract
task of recognizing the proper structural components of the
system M, that our native perception and intuition fail us.

The task of replacing this intuition by some precisely defined mathematical operation has been tackled in a number of
ways.[2] Many of them are worth examining, if for no better
reason than that they will illustrate and deepen our conception
of the task. One, which perhaps comes closest to what we
want, simply divides M into those subsets which are connected
by as few links of L as possible, thus leaving as many of the
links as possible within the subsystems.[3] However, neither
this nor any other of the existing methods is exactly suited
to the conditions which confront us in this case. I shall now
try to show that we can develop a well-defined criterion for
decomposition, simply by thinking carefully about the relation between a design program and its realization.

Let us think just what the successful realization of the
program demands. Fundamentally, it demands that the sets
in the program have two kinds of property, which we may
illustrate by taking the typical piece of a program shown
below. S_1 and S_2 are two different sets of requirements. S_3
contains all the requirements in S_1 and S_2 together.

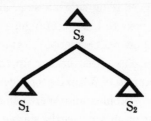

First we must be able to find constructive diagrams for S_1 and S_2 individually. This means that the misfits which S_1 contains must cohere somehow, and suggest a physical aspect or component of the form under consideration; and the same for S_2.

Secondly, if the decomposition is to serve any useful purpose, it must not be necessary to construct the diagram for S_3 from scratch. Instead, it must be possible to derive a constructive diagram for S_3 in some simple way from the diagrams already constructed for S_1 and S_2 in isolation.

To put it simply, the first of these conditions depends on the internal structure of the sets S_1 and S_2, while the second deals with the relations between these two sets.

Let us take the two conditions in order.

What is it about the internal structure of any problem that makes it hard to solve? In nine cases out of ten, we cannot solve it, because we cannot grasp it; we cannot see what the internal structure is "driving at." The subproblems we are considering here, because they are made up of sets of requirements that have been isolated from the rest of the design problem they belong to, show this acutely. Take two misfits at random. "The kettle must be comfortable for the hand to hold," and "The kettle must be economical to heat," which we should probably consider as noninteracting. These two define a two-element subset of M for the kettle problem. It is hard to see, however, what these two elements have in common, or indeed whether this set, taken by itself, means anything.

If the set M contains m misfits, there are 2^m possible subsets of M, and so 2^m subsidiary problems. Any design problem of practical interest and complexity will probably contain at least as many as 100 variables, and will therefore have 2^{100} or roughly 10^{30} (1,000,000,000,000,000,000,000,000,000,000) different subsets of variables. Almost each one of these subsets will be hard to grasp, because, as in the example of the two-element subset just given, it will not be clear what its rather disparate member-variables "have in common."

Our natural reaction to this is to look for those very rare sets of variables with integrity in which the variables do "have something in common," so that they do make sense.

The use of verbal concepts is an efficient artificial way of finding sets which have something in common. Certain issues which appear in our analysis as subsets of M, happen to be tied together by familiar words; as a result everyone comes to be able to manipulate these sets, can understand what he is dealing with, and can therefore get to grips with the issues the set represents.

Unfortunately, the sets of misfits identified by verbal concepts do not have any special functional significance, and do not usually lend themselves particularly well to interpretation through constructive diagrams. A constructive diagram requires that the requirements it represents have some physical implications in common. From this point of view, it is easy to see that not all the possible subsets of M will be equally easy to diagram constructively. We may put this another way, perhaps, by saying that some subsets open up physical possibilities more readily than others. Some sets of misfits, in view of their interactions, seem naturally to belong together, and, taken as units, suggest physical form very strongly. Others will seem to have no special reason for being sets, and are not especially easy to diagram, and do not really "belong" to the problem.

If we are to make anything sensible of the subsets in this program, we must now ask just which sets of points to consider as being the most "diagrammable." This depends on the pattern of interactions between the misfits. Where, after all, does the interaction among the requirements spring from? It springs from the intractable nature of the available materials and the conditions under which the form has to be made. Two misfits are seen to interact only because, in some sense at least, they deal with the same kind of physical consideration. If they dealt with utterly different aspects, there could be no basis either for conflict or for concurrence.

In building, the need for acoustic insulation conflicts with the need to build with easily transportable prefabricated materials. These two needs conflict because the first calls for massive inert walls, while the second calls for light walls. The physical feature of the world their interaction depends on is mass. Again, in a highway, the need for safety on curves conflicts with the need to keep land costs down, because the wider the curves have to be for safety's sake, the larger the area eaten up by the transition curves at interchanges. In this case the interaction between the two requirements depends on the radius of the curve.

It is such a physical center of implication, if I may call it that, which the designer finds it easy to grasp. Because it refers to a distinguishable physical property or entity, it can be expressed diagrammatically, and provides a possible nonverbal point of entry into the problem. If we can find sets of variables in which there are specially dense interactions, we may assume, in these cases, that the density of the interaction resides in a particularly strong identifiable physical aspect of the problem. These sets will be the easiest of all to grasp constructively. Thus:

If, therefore, we break the problem apart in such a way that its clusters of variables are as richly connected, internally, as possible, we shall have clues to those physical aspects of the problem which play the most important functional part in the problem and are therefore most likely to furnish handles for the designer's comprehension. These are the sets which will be the easiest to diagram.

If we are to solve the problem M by working our way through the program, solving various subproblems separately, it must obviously be possible to put the resulting diagrams together somehow when we have them. This is the second condition a successful program must satisfy. But it will only be possible to fuse two diagrams under very special circumstances. Why, for instance, can we not simply make a diagram for each separate variable, so that we get m diagrams, and superimpose these m diagrams somehow? The reason is obvious. The physical characteristics demanded by one requirement conflict with the physical characteristics demanded by another. This is, in fact, exactly what we mean by saying that two misfit variables conflict. The same is true of more complex diagrams. We have already drawn attention to the fact that a subset which contained all the economic variables and no others, for example, would be comparatively useless, because its economic implications conflict too strongly with the other implications of the problem. Naturally if the diagram for the economic requirements is not going to be compatible with that for the comfort requirements, say, there is no point in constructing the two diagrams independently.

How shall we meet this difficulty? At all events, we cannot avoid encountering the conflicts somewhere in the program. No matter in what order we consider the requirements, if we are to find a form which satisfies them all, we must at some stage resolve each one of the conflicts. But if we think about it, we see that the difficulty of resolving them is different at different stages of the process of realization. At the beginning of the process, the sets of requirements we apply ourselves to are still small enough for their implications to be carried in the mind's eye; and these implications are therefore not yet frozen in any explicit diagrammatic form; they are still flexible enough to be successfully integrated with one another in spite of conflicts. The further along in the process we are, the more our thoughts about these implications have been forced by their complexity to become concrete, whether diagrammatically or conceptually, and the more their rigidity resists further modification. As a result, the later in the process conflicting diagrams have to be integrated, the more difficult the integration is.

Naturally, then, since the conflicts have to be resolved sooner or later, we should like to meet them as early in the process of realization as we can, while our ideas are still flexible. From this point of view, the fewer links there are between the major subsets of the decomposition, the better. Ideally, we should like to find a first partition of M like this, for instance, where no links are cut by the partition, though this will not in practice usually be possible.[4]

The need for subsets we can grasp diagrammatically calls for sets of variables whose *internal* interactions are very rich. The need to resolve the conflicts between the diagrams we get from them calls for as little interaction *between* subsets as possible. Clearly these two are compatible; indeed, they can be expressed jointly as follows.

Consider just one level of the decomposition, where some set S is to be partitioned into disjoint subsets $(S_1, S_2 \cdots S_\alpha \cdots S_\mu)$. We wish to choose these S_α in such a way that we can invent a constructive diagram for S_1 whose implications will not later turn out to be hopelessly contradicted by an independently conceived diagram for one of the other S_α; and the same for S_2, S_3, etcetera. Why is this difficult to do in terms of the variables' behavior?

It is difficult because any variables which are linked exercise mutual constraint over one another's states. If we fix the values of the variables of S_1, the values which the variables of the other S_α can take are already constrained to some extent by the probabilistic links which bind them to this S_1. In other words, the values which the variables of S_1 take, tell us something about the values which the variables in the other S_α can take; they give us information. The sparser the links between the S_α, the less the values of the variables in S_1 can tell us about the values in S_2, etc.; the less information the links carry across the partition, the freer we are to construct a diagram for S_2 once we have fixed the solution of S_1 in our minds.

If we wish to construct a diagram for S_1 first, say, and then wish to construct a compatible diagram for S_2 independently, we want to be free to manipulate the values of the variables in S_2 without this manipulation being constrained by the fact that the variables of S_1 are now held constant in our minds, by the diagrammatic expression invented for them. To achieve this, we must choose the S_α in such a way that the variables in different subsets of the partition exercise as little informational constraint on one another as possible.

As shown in Appendix 2, the conditions specified in Chapter 8 define a unique probability distribution $p(\lambda)$ over the states λ of any set of variables S.[5] Appendix 2 then shows that, given any partition π of a set S into subsets, $\pi\{S_1 \cdots S_\mu\}$, we may establish a measure of information transfer or informational dependence among these subsets, called $R(\pi)$.[6] Since this $R(\pi)$ is defined for all possible partitions of any S, we may obtain the desired decomposition of the set M, by minimizing $R(\pi)$ for successive partitions of M and its descendants.

Thus, we first find that partition of M, $\pi(M)$, for which

$R(\pi)$ is minimum. This establishes the first level of the decomposition, thus, say:

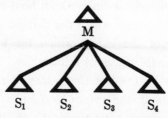

We then apply the same method to the sets S_α: we look for that partition $\pi(S_1)$ of S_1, for which $R(\pi)$ is minimum, and similarly for $S_2 \cdots$, thus obtaining the second level of the decomposition. We continue with this procedure iteratively, until we reach a level of decomposition at which all the sets contain one variable only. (Condition 4 of Chapter 6, page 82.)

The tree of sets this decomposition gives is, within the terms of this book, a complete structural description of the design problem defined by M; and it therefore serves as a program for the synthesis of a form which solves this problem.

Let us remember the properties of the program.

1. The tree is, in its hierarchical form, the same as any other hierarchy of concepts — except that the concepts are here defined extensionally as sets of variables, rather than intensionally by meaning.

2. The particular tree arrived at by the method outlined gives an explicit description of the structure implicitly responsible for the success and stability of the unselfconscious form-making process.

3. The tree gives the strongest possible decomposition of the problem that does not interfere with the task

of synthesizing its parts in a unified way. Each subsidiary problem it defines has its own integrity, and is as independent as it can be of the rest of the problem.

4. We must remember that the hierarchy of sets which the tree defines will not always be easy to understand. Even in some of the smaller sets which contain only half a dozen variables, these variables will often seem disparate, and their juxtaposition may be startling. The relevance of each variable is only to be properly understood after careful examination of its functional relation to the other variables in the set. Since the potential coherence of such a set of variables comes from its physical implications, it can only be grasped graphically, by means of a constructive diagram that brings out these implications. Each diagram for a set S must do two things:

As a requirement diagram:

    a. It must bring out just those features of the problem which are relevant to this set of requirements.

    b. It must include no information which is not explicitly called for by these requirements.

As a form diagram:

    a. It must be so specific that it has all the physical characteristics called for by the requirements of S.

    b. Yet it must be so general that it contains no arbitrary characteristics, and so summarizes, abstractly, the nature of every form which might satisfy S.

Above all, the designer must resist the temptation to summarize the contents of the tree in terms of well-known verbal concepts. He must not expect to be able to see for every S some verbal paradigm like "This one deals with the acoustic aspects of the form." If he tries to do that, he denies the whole purpose of the analysis, by allowing verbal preconceptions to interfere with the pattern which the program shows him. The effect of the design program is that each set of requirements draws his attention to just one major physical and functional issue, rather than to some verbal or preconceived issue. It thereby forces him to consolidate the physical ideas present in his mind as seedlings, and to make physical order out of them.

To finish this section I give an example of the way a set of requirements, when taken together, create a new idea about what one main feature of a physical form ought to be. Consider the design of the now familiar one-hole kettle. The single wide short spout embraces a number of requirements: all those which center round the problems of getting water in and out of the kettle, the problem of doing it safely without the lid's falling off, the problem of making manufacture as simple as possible, the problem of providing warning when the kettle boils, the need for internal maintenance. In the old kettles these requirements were met separately by three components: a spout for pouring, a hole in the top for filling and cleaning, and a top which kept the steam in and rattled when the kettle boiled. Suddenly, when it became possible to put non-corrosive metals on the market, and cheap, available descaler made it unnecessary to get into the kettle for descaling, it became apparent that all these requirements really had a single center of physical implication, not three. The wide spout can be used for filling and pouring, and as a whistle, and there is no top to fall open and let scalding water out over the pourer's hands. The set of requirements, once its unity is recognized, leads to a single physical component of the kettle.

The program, which represents a functional decomposition of the problem, is a way of identifying the problem's major functional aspects. But what kind of physical form, exactly, is the designer likely to realize with the help of such a program? Let us look at the form problem from the beginning.

The organization of any complex physical object is hierarchical. It is true that, if we wish, we may dismiss this observation as an hallucination caused by the way the human brain, being disposed to see in terms of articulations and hierarchies, perceives the world. On the whole, though, there are good reasons to believe in the hierarchical subdivision of the world as an objective feature of reality. Indeed, many scientists, trying to understand the physical world, find that they have first to identify its physical components, much as I have argued in these notes for isolating the abstract components of a problem. To understand the human body you need to know what to consider as its principal functional and structural divisions. You cannot understand it until you recognize the nervous system, the hormonal system, the vasomotor system, the heart, the arms, legs, trunk, head, and so on as entities.[7] You cannot understand chemistry without knowing the pieces of which molecules are made. You cannot claim to have much understanding of the universe until you recognize its galaxies as important pieces. You cannot understand the modern city until you know that although roads are physically intertwined with the distribution of services, the two remain functionally distinct.

Scientists try to identify the components of existing structure. Designers try to shape the components of new structures. The search for the right components, and the right way to build the form up from these components, is the greatest physical challenge faced by the designer. I believe that if the hierarchical program is intelligently used, it offers the key to this very basic problem — and will actually point to the major physical components of which the form should consist.

When we consider the kinds of constructive diagram which are likely to be suggested by sets of requirements, at first it seems that the nature of these diagrams is very various. Some diagrams seem to define overall pattern properties of the form, like being circular, being low rather than high, being homogeneous. Other diagrams seem to be piecelike rather than patternlike. They define pieces of which the whole form is made, like a diagram defining the street as a piece of the city, or the handle as a piece of the kettle, and so on.

Actually the distinction between patternlike and piecelike diagrams is more apparent than real. Take a simple example, a diagram which specifies a circular plan. Being circular is usually thought of as an overall property of a plan. But the plan's being circular may also be guaranteed by a surrounding wall or boundary of some sort. In other words, we can invest what is apparently a pattern property in a component which is much more of a piece: namely the boundary.

This is the general rule. Every aspect of a form, whether piecelike or patternlike, can be understood as a structure of components. Every object is a hierarchy of components, the large ones specifying the pattern of distribution of the smaller ones, the small ones themselves, though at first sight more clearly piecelike, in fact again patterns specifying the arrangement and distribution of still smaller components.

Every component has this twofold nature: it is first a unit, and second a pattern, both a pattern and a unit. Its nature as a unit makes it an entity distinct from its surroundings. Its nature as a pattern specifies the arrangement of its own component units. It is the culmination of the designer's task to make every diagram both a pattern and a unit. As a unit it will fit into the hierarchy of larger components that fall above it; as a pattern it will specify the hierarchy of smaller components which it itself is made of.

The hierarchical composition of these diagrams will then lead to a physical object whose structural hierarchy is the exact counterpart of the functional hierarchy established during the analysis of the problem; as the program clarifies the component *sources* of the form's structure, so its realization, in parallel, will actually begin to define the form's *physical* components and their hierarchical organization.[8]

My main task has been to show that there is a deep and important underlying structural correspondence between the pattern of a problem and the process of designing a physical form which answers that problem. I believe that the great architect has in the past always been aware of the patterned similarity of problem and process, and that it is only the sense of this similarity of structure that ever led him to the design of great forms.

The same pattern is implicit in the action of the unselfconscious form-producing system, and responsible for its success. But before we can ourselves turn a problem into form, because we are selfconscious, we need to make explicit maps of the problem's structure, and therefore need first to invent a conceptual framework for such maps. This is all that I have tried to do.

Since my effort may well meet with resistance, I like to see the few steps taken here reflected in a parable of an imaginary past society.

Suppose there was once a people who had no formalized arithmetic. When they wanted what we think of as arithmetical results, they got them by guessing. So if they wished to know the area of a corn patch they paced its two sides (six paces by ten paces, say), and then mulled the two numbers over. Eventually one of them came up with an answer — he would say some number, that is, which estimated the bags of corn needed to sow that patch. He might say 60, 61, 58, whatever occurred to him. (If we were in such a situation we should form what we call the prod-

uct of the two numbers, 60, and determine the amount of corn needed in terms of this area.)

It is easy to see that the people of this imaginary society might not have found formal arithmetic acceptable. Their own method was usually not too far off the mark (sowing corn is such a loose test, anyway, that what we call inaccuracy would not have been noticeable) — and besides, there was something rather noble about the seers (magicians?) who performed the tasks of "calculation." Some men were better at it than others, certainly; some had the power to produce appropriate answers, some produced answers rather wider of the mark. But that didn't seem to matter. Instead the power was regarded as a great human gift, the people who possessed it were honored for their capability. And both these seers themselves and their admirers opposed the introduction of a formalized arithmetic most rigidly, did not see the possible developments, were interested only in preserving their own limited capacities for calculation.

Such resistance was not altogether foolish either. There were wise men, too, among those who opposed arithmetic. They foresaw, correctly, the materialism which it would induce. Its very first achievement, once introduced, would be to make calculation more precise and easier, and thereby to save corn. And soon number and economy and size would dominate the human being. The immediate good done by the formulation of arithmetic would be small, and not worth taking risks for on its own account.

What neither the wise men nor the seers foresaw, however, was the miraculous developments that this formulation later led to. By first understanding the shape of the technique which produced the form of the result, man found further insight. He found that it is not only the result which is important, but the process too. Not only the form of the results, but the form of the path which led to them. It was only by questioning the foundations of geometry and the processes of geometrical proof that Riemann *invented the geometry which later became the basis for Einstein's theory of relativity. Other great theorems are possible today because multiplication and addition were once defined. It was only because man gave thought to the seemingly obvious processes which underlay arithmetic that he was able to refine mathematics, and able to proceed to forms of still higher order, mathematical shapes of greater elegance and fuller understanding.*

The shapes of mathematics are abstract, of course, and the shapes of architecture concrete and human. But that difference is inessential. The crucial quality of shape, no matter of what kind, lies in its organization, and when we think of it this way we call it form. Man's feeling for mathematical form was able to develop only from his feeling for the processes of proof. I believe that our feeling for architectural form can never reach a comparable order of development, until we too have first learned a comparable feeling for the process of design.

APPENDICES

Here is a worked example, taken from a recent paper, "The Determination of Components for an Indian Village." * The problem treated is this. An agricultural village of six hundred people is to be reorganized to make it fit present and future conditions developing in rural India.

The set M, which follows, contains all the misfit variables that are pertinent to the organization of the village. All these misfit variables are stated here in their positive form; that is, as needs or requirements which must be satisfied positively in a properly functioning village. They are, however, all derived from statements about potential misfits: each one represents some aspect of the village which could go wrong, and is therefore a misfit variable in the terms of Chapter 2.

M includes variables which represent three different kinds of need:

(1) all those which are explicitly felt by villagers themselves as needs,

(2) all those which are called for by national and regional economy and social purpose, and

(3) all those already satisfied implicitly in the present village (which are required, though not felt as needs by anybody).

(The headings on the left are for convenience in the listing stage only, and play no part in the subsequent analysis.)

* In Christopher Jones, ed., *Conference on Design Method* (Oxford: Pergamon, 1963). My lists and diagrams are reproduced here by kind permission of Pergamon Press.

Religion and Caste

1. Harijans regarded as ritually impure, untouchable, etc.
2. Proper disposal of dead.
3. Rules about house door not facing south.
4. Certain water and certain trees are thought of as sacred.
5. Provision for festivals and religious meetings.
6. Wish for temples.
7. Cattle treated as sacred, and vegetarian attitude.
8. Members of castes maintain their caste profession as far as possible.
9. Members of one caste like to be together and separate from others, and will not eat or drink together.
10. Need for elaborate weddings.

Social Forces

11. Marriage is to person from another village.
12. Extended family is in one house.
13. Family solidarity and neighborliness even after separation.
14. Economic integration of village on payment-in-kind basis.
15. Modern move toward payment in cash.
16. Women gossip extensively while bathing, fetching water, on way to field latrines, etc.
17. Village has fixed men's social groups.
18. Need to divide land among sons of successive generations.
19. People want to own land personally.
20. People of different factions prefer to have no contact.
21. Eradication of untouchability.
22. Abolition of Zamindari and uneven land distribution.
23. Men's groups chatting, smoking, even late at night.
24. Place for village events — dancing, plays, singing, etc., wrestling.
25. Assistance for physically handicapped, aged, widows.
26. Sentimental system: wish not to destroy old way of life; love of present habits governing bathing, food, etc.

27. Family is authoritarian.
28. Proper boundaries of ownership and maintenance responsibility.
29. Provision for daily bath, segregated by sex, caste, and age.

Agriculture

30. Efficient and rapid distribution of seeds, fertilizer, etc., from block HQ.
31. Efficient distribution of fertilizer, manure, seed, from village storage to fields.
32. Reclamation and use of uncultivated land.
33. Fertile land to be used to best advantage.
34. Full collection of natural manure (animal and human).
35. Protection of crops from insects, weeds, disease.
36. Protection of crops from thieves, cattle, goats, monkeys, etc.
37. Provision of storage for distributing and marketing crops.
38. Provision of threshing floor and its protection from marauders.
39. Best cotton and cash crop.
40. Best food grain crop.
41. Good vegetable crop.
42. Efficient plowing, weeding, harvesting, leveling.
43. Consolidation of land.
44. Crops must be brought home from fields.
45. Development of horticulture.
46. Respect for traditional agricultural practices.
47. Need for new implements when old ones are damaged, etc.
48. Scarcity of land.
49. Cooperative farming.

Animal Husbandry

50. Protected storage of fodder.
51. Improve quality of fodder available.
52. Improve quantity of fodder available.
53. Upgrading of cattle.
54. Provision for feeding cattle.
55. Cattle access to water.

56. Sheltered accommodation for cattle (sleeping, milking, feeding).
57. Protection of cattle from disease.
58. Development of other animal industry.
59. Efficient use and marketing of dairy products.
60. Minimize the use of animal traction to take pressure off shortage.

Employment

61. Sufficient fluid employment for laborers temporarily (seasonally) out of work.
62. Provision of cottage industry and artisan workshops and training.
63. Development of village industry.
64. Simplify the mobility of labor, to and from villages, and to and from fields and industries and houses.
65. Diversification of villages' economic base — not all occupations agricultural.
66. Efficient provision and use of power.

Water

67. Drinking water to be good, sweet.
68. Easy access to drinking water.
69. Fullest possible irrigation benefit derived from available water.
70. Full collection of underground water for irrigation.
71. Full collection of monsoon water for use.
72. Prevent famine if monsoon fails.
73. Conservation of water resources for future.
74. Maintenance of irrigation facilities.
75. Drainage of land to prevent waterlogging, etc.
76. Flood control to protect houses, roads, etc.

Material Welfare

77. Village and individual houses must be protected from fire.
78. Shade for sitting and walking.
79. Provision of cool breeze.
80. Security for cattle.

81. Security for women and children.
82. Provision for children to play (under supervision).
83. In summer people sleep in open.
84. Accommodation for panchayat records, meetings, etc.
85. Everyone's accommodation for sitting and sleeping should be protected from rain.
86. No overcrowding.
87. Safe storage of goods.
88. Place to wash and dry clothes.
89. Provision of goods, for sale.
90. Better provision for preparing meals.
91. Provision and storage of fuel.
92. House has to be cleaned, washed, drained.
93. Lighting.

Transportation

94. Provision for animal traffic.
95. Access to bus as near as possible.
96. Access to railway station.
97. Minimize transportation costs for bulk produce (grain, potatoes, etc.).
98. Daily produce requires cheap and constant (monsoon) access to market.
99. Industry requires strong transportation support.
100. Provision for bicycle age in every village by 1965.
101. Pedestrian traffic within village.
102. Accommodation for processions.
103. Bullock cart access to house for bulk of grain, fodder.

Forests and Soils

104. Plant ecology to be kept healthy.
105. Insufficient forest land.
106. Young trees need protection from goats, etc.
107. Soil conservation.
108. Road and dwelling erosion.
109. Reclamation of eroded land, gullies, etc.
110. Prevent land erosion.

Education

111. Provision for primary education.
112. Access to a secondary school.
113. Good attendance in school.
114. Development of women's independent activities.
115. Opportunity for youth activities.
116. Improvement of adult literacy.
117. Spread of information about birth control, disease, etc.
118. Demonstration projects which spread by example.
119. Efficient use of school; no distraction of students.

Health

120. Curative measures for disease available to villagers.
121. Facilities for birth, pre- and post-natal care, birth control.
122. Disposal of human excreta.
123. Prevent breeding germs and disease starters.
124. Prevent spread of human disease by carriers, infection, contagion.
125. Prevent malnutrition.

Implementation

126. Close contact with village-level worker.
127. Contact with block development officer and extension officers.
128. Price assurance for crops.
129. Factions refuse to cooperate or agree.
130. Need for increased incentives and aspirations.
131. Panchayat must have more power and respect.
132. Need to develop projects which benefit from government subsidies.

Regional, Political, and National Development

133. Social integration with neighboring villages.
134. Wish to keep up with achievements of neighboring villages.
135. Spread of official information about taxes, elections, etc.

136. Accommodation of wandering caste groups, incoming labor, etc.
137. Radio communication.
138. Achieve economic independence so as not to strain national transportation and resources.
139. Proper connection with bridges, roads, hospitals, schools, proposed at the district level.
140. Develop rural community spirit: destroy selfishness, isolationism.
141. Prevent migration of young people and harijans to cities.

This defines the set M.

The links between these misfit variables are tabulated below. For the sake of simplicity, I allowed only one strength of link, so that $\nu = 1$, and for every pair of variables $\nu_{ij} = 0, 1,$ or -1. Further, the signs of the links are not indicated: as we shall see in Appendix 2, the decomposition turns out to be independent of the link signs. The table below simply shows those linked pairs of variables for which $\nu_{ij} = 1$ or -1.

1 interacts with 8, 9, 12, 13, 14, 21, 28, 29, 48, 61, 67, 68, 70, 77, 86, 101, 106, 113, 124, 140, 141.

2 interacts with 3, 4, 6, 26, 29, 32, 52, 71, 98, 102, 105, 123, 133.

3 interacts with 2, 12, 13, 17, 26, 76, 78, 79, 88, 101, 103, 119.

4 interacts with 2, 5, 6, 17, 29, 32, 45, 56, 63, 71, 74, 78, 79, 88, 91, 105, 106, 110, 124.

5 interacts with 4, 6, 10, 14, 17, 21, 24, 46, 102, 113, 116, 118, 131, 133, 140.

6 interacts with 2, 4, 5, 20, 21, 53, 58, 61, 63, 82, 102, 111, 117, 130, 134, 135.

7 interacts with 20, 31, 34, 53, 57, 58, 59, 80, 85, 86, 94, 105, 106, 123, 124, 125.

8 interacts with 1, 9, 14, 15, 21, 22, 25, 27, 48, 58, 59, 61, 62, 63, 64, 65, 89, 95, 96, 99, 111, 112, 114, 115, 116, 121, 129, 136, 140, 141.

9 interacts with 1, 8, 11, 12, 13, 15, 17, 18, 20, 21, 28, 29, 36, 43, 49, 56, 62, 64, 80, 81, 101, 113, 118, 124, 129, 136, 140, 141.

10 interacts with 5, 13, 14, 15, 18, 24, 26, 65, 68, 93, 102, 134.

11 interacts with 9, 12, 64, 95, 96, 114, 133, 134.

12 interacts with 1, 3, 9, 11, 17, 18, 19, 25, 26, 28, 34, 36, 41, 43, 49, 56, 62, 63, 76, 80, 81, 85, 86, 87, 90, 91, 93, 121, 122, 129, 140, 141.

13 interacts with 1, 3, 9, 10, 17, 20, 25, 28, 33, 34, 36, 37, 41, 45, 56, 62, 68, 79, 80, 81, 83, 86, 91, 94, 101, 106, 108, 121, 122, 129, 137, 140, 141.

14 interacts with 1, 5, 8, 10, 15, 19, 20, 21, 28, 30, 40, 43, 44, 47, 54, 62, 63, 64, 65, 86, 97, 121, 129, 130, 133, 138, 141.

15 interacts with 8, 9, 10, 14, 18, 21, 22, 37, 39, 41, 44, 45, 46, 58, 59, 61, 62, 63, 64, 65, 66, 95, 96, 97, 98, 112, 116, 125, 127, 128, 129, 130, 132, 133, 135, 137, 138, 141.

16 interacts with 27, 29, 34, 68, 78, 79, 82, 88, 95, 101, 114, 117, 119, 122.

17 interacts with 3, 4, 5, 9, 12, 13, 20, 23, 27, 37, 38, 43, 49, 65, 69, 80, 81, 86, 89, 101, 110, 115, 116, 117, 118, 126, 129, 135.

18 interacts with 9, 10, 12, 15, 19, 26, 28, 31, 33, 42, 43, 44, 47, 48, 49, 60, 65, 69, 70, 74, 77, 79, 85, 97, 98, 103, 110, 140, 141.

19 interacts with 12, 14, 18, 22, 26, 28, 32, 33, 36, 37, 38, 41, 45, 49, 69, 71, 86, 104, 106, 107, 110, 118, 126, 140.

20 interacts with 6, 9, 13, 14, 17, 24, 29, 30, 36, 37, 43, 54, 64, 68, 80, 84, 89, 102, 116, 117, 129, 131, 133, 140.

21 interacts with 1, 5, 6, 8, 9, 14, 15, 24, 61, 63, 89, 95, 96, 111, 112, 113, 115, 116, 137, 139, 140, 141.

22 interacts with 8, 15, 19, 31, 32, 33, 36, 42, 44, 47, 49, 60, 61, 64, 69, 71, 74, 97, 98, 104, 107, 110, 127, 140.

23 interacts with 4, 17, 31, 34, 62, 63, 71, 76, 78, 79, 82, 83, 93, 95, 100, 101, 105, 115, 116, 119, 126, 132, 137.

24 interacts with 5, 10, 20, 21, 38, 82, 93, 100, 101, 102, 108, 115, 130, 133, 135, 140, 141.

25 interacts with 8, 12, 13, 26, 27, 36, 62, 81, 90, 92, 111, 114, 116, 120.

26 interacts with 2, 3, 10, 12, 18, 19, 25, 29, 31, 33, 34, 41, 53, 56, 58, 62, 67, 68, 76, 85, 90, 91, 92, 93, 108, 113, 122, 123, 124, 130.

27 interacts with 8, 16, 17, 25, 29, 62, 68, 81, 86, 88, 90, 92, 113, 114, 122, 130.

28 interacts with 1, 9, 12, 13, 14, 18, 19, 29, 31, 33, 34, 35, 36, 37, 38, 42, 45, 49, 50, 54, 55, 56, 62, 74, 92, 103, 106, 107, 108, 109, 110, 118, 127, 129, 131.

29 interacts with 1, 2, 4, 9, 16, 20, 26, 27, 28, 41, 67, 71, 81, 85, 88, 92, 101, 119, 122, 124.

30 interacts with 7, 14, 20, 31, 33, 35, 40, 47, 63, 95, 97, 98, 107, 126, 127, 129, 130, 131, 132, 133, 139.

31 interacts with 7, 18, 22, 23, 26, 28, 30, 33, 34, 35, 37, 40, 43, 44, 49, 50, 52, 54, 59, 60, 80, 89, 94, 98, 106, 107, 109, 128, 131, 132.

32 interacts with 2, 4, 19, 22, 34, 42, 43, 46, 48, 52, 54, 60, 61, 63, 65, 69, 70, 71, 73, 74, 75, 104, 105, 107, 109, 110, 122, 129.

33 interacts with 13, 18, 19, 22, 26, 28, 30, 31, 34, 35, 36, 41, 54, 56, 59, 74, 78, 80, 90, 91, 92, 94, 105, 107, 118, 122, 123, 124, 136.

34 interacts with 7, 12, 13, 16, 23, 26, 28, 31, 32, 33, 41, 54, 56, 59, 74, 78, 80, 90, 91, 92, 94, 105, 107, 118, 122, 123, 124, 136.

35 interacts with 28, 30, 31, 33, 39, 42, 43, 46, 61, 79, 104, 118, 137.

36 interacts with 9, 12, 13, 19, 20, 22, 25, 28, 33, 38, 40, 41, 43, 45, 52, 54, 61, 68, 80, 81, 86, 94, 106, 110, 136.

37 interacts with 13, 15, 17, 19, 20, 28, 31, 38, 43, 44, 49, 50, 72, 76, 97, 103, 128, 133, 140.

38 interacts with 17, 19, 24, 28, 36, 37, 40, 42, 43, 44, 50, 52, 58, 61, 68, 76, 78, 79, 94, 97, 106, 128.

39 interacts with 15, 33, 35, 44, 48, 62, 69, 70, 72, 75, 97, 104, 118, 127, 134, 137, 138.

40 interacts with 14, 30, 31, 33, 36, 38, 42, 44, 48, 69, 70, 97, 104, 107, 118, 125, 127, 134, 137, 138.

41 interacts with 12, 13, 15, 19, 26, 29, 33, 34, 36, 44, 48, 51, 65, 69, 70, 71, 72, 92, 98, 104, 107, 118, 122, 125, 127, 138.

42 interacts with 18, 22, 28, 32, 33, 35, 38, 40, 43, 48, 49, 50, 57, 69, 104, 105, 107, 110, 118, 137.

43 interacts with 9, 12, 14, 17, 18, 20, 31, 32, 33, 35, 36, 37, 38, 42, 48, 51, 60, 64, 69, 71, 86, 101, 104, 107, 109, 119, 129, 140.

44 interacts with 14, 15, 18, 22, 31, 37, 38, 39, 40, 41, 51, 52, 60, 62, 87, 97, 98, 110.

45 interacts with 4, 13, 15, 19, 28, 36, 48, 54, 65, 69, 70, 71, 73, 74, 78, 79, 91, 104, 105, 106, 110, 118, 125, 127, 130, 138.

46 interacts with 5, 15, 32, 33, 35, 47, 66, 106, 107, 118, 130.

47 interacts with 14, 18, 22, 30, 33, 46, 62, 107, 118, 130.

48 interacts with 1, 8, 18, 32, 33, 39, 40, 41, 42, 43, 45, 52, 63, 71, 75, 85, 86, 97, 99, 105, 107, 109, 110, 119, 129, 130, 141.

49 interacts with 9, 12, 17, 18, 19, 22, 28, 31, 37, 42, 51, 64, 68, 86, 97, 107, 110, 117, 118, 128, 129, 130, 132, 133, 138, 140.

50 interacts with 28, 31, 37, 38, 42, 52, 54, 60, 76, 77, 85, 87, 94, 103.

51 interacts with 33, 41, 43, 44, 49, 53, 54, 59, 69, 77, 104, 107, 118, 127, 136.

52 interacts with 2, 31, 32, 36, 38, 44, 48, 50, 53, 54, 59, 71, 91, 104, 106, 107, 136.

53 interacts with 6, 7, 26, 51, 52, 56, 57, 59, 60, 66, 72, 118, 126, 127, 137.

54 interacts with 14, 20, 28, 31, 32, 33, 34, 36, 45, 50, 51, 52, 56, 57, 59, 71, 80, 91, 94, 106, 107, 110, 115.

55 interacts with 28, 67, 68, 71, 80, 119, 123, 124.

56 interacts with 4, 9, 12, 13, 26, 28, 34, 53, 54, 57, 59, 76, 78, 80, 85, 86, 92, 102, 123, 124.

57 interacts with 7, 42, 53, 54, 56, 59, 60, 70, 86, 94, 117, 118, 123, 126, 127, 137.

58 interacts with 6, 7, 8, 15, 26, 38, 65, 72, 76, 78, 93, 96, 98, 99, 125, 127, 130, 138.

59 interacts with 7, 8, 15, 31, 34, 51, 52, 53, 54, 57, 58, 60, 65, 66, 72, 96, 98, 99, 125, 127, 130, 138.

60 interacts with 18, 22, 31, 32, 43, 44, 50, 53, 57, 59, 91, 94, 97, 98, 103, 131.

61 interacts with 1, 6, 8, 15, 21, 22, 32, 35, 36, 38, 63, 74, 86, 95, 96, 97, 98, 99, 105, 108, 109, 110, 119, 120, 127, 131, 139, 140, 141.

62 interacts with 8, 9, 12, 13, 14, 15, 23, 25, 26, 27, 28, 39, 44, 47, 65, 66, 72, 85, 86, 87, 89, 93, 114, 115, 116, 119, 127, 130, 132, 138, 141.

63 interacts with 4, 6, 8, 12, 14, 15, 21, 23, 30, 32, 48, 61, 64, 65, 66, 68, 70, 71, 72, 75, 86, 93, 96, 99, 100, 116, 119, 127, 129, 130, 132, 133, 134, 136, 138, 140, 141.

64 interacts with 8, 9, 11, 14, 15, 20, 22, 43, 49, 63, 81, 85, 86, 95, 99, 100, 101, 109, 112, 113, 127, 130, 133, 136, 139.

65 interacts with 8, 10, 14, 15, 17, 18, 32, 41, 45, 58, 59, 62, 63, 66, 72, 84, 99, 111, 114, 116, 127, 130, 133, 134, 138, 139, 141.

66 interacts with 15, 46, 53, 59, 62, 63, 65, 68, 70, 71, 75, 93, 130, 132, 133, 137, 139, 141.

67 interacts with 1, 26, 29, 55, 76, 86, 92, 122, 123.

68 interacts with 1, 10, 13, 16, 20, 26, 27, 36, 38, 49, 55, 63, 66, 71, 86, 94, 101, 109, 110, 114, 119, 124, 129, 131, 132, 141.

69 interacts with 17, 18, 19, 22, 32, 33, 39, 40, 41, 42, 43, 45, 51, 74, 75, 92, 104, 105, 107, 132.

70 interacts with 1, 18, 32, 33, 39, 40, 41, 45, 57, 63, 66, 71, 72, 73, 86, 104, 110, 131, 132.

71 interacts with 2, 4, 19, 22, 23, 29, 32, 33, 41, 43, 45, 48, 52, 54, 55, 63, 66, 68, 70, 73, 75, 76, 79, 88, 98, 104, 105, 107, 108, 109, 110, 120, 129, 131, 132, 133.

72 interacts with 33, 37, 39, 41, 53, 58, 59, 62, 63, 65, 70, 104, 128, 130, 131.

73 interacts with 32, 45, 70, 71, 78, 91, 104, 105, 108, 109, 110.

74 interacts with 4, 18, 22, 28, 32, 33, 34, 45, 61, 69, 105, 107, 109, 110, 127.

75 interacts with 32, 33, 39, 48, 63, 66, 69, 71, 98, 100, 104, 107, 123, 124, 133.

76 interacts with 3, 12, 23, 26, 37, 38, 50, 56, 58, 67, 71, 85, 87, 90, 91, 92, 95, 98, 101, 108, 113, 120, 122, 123, 124, 127.

77 interacts with 1, 18, 50, 51, 79, 83, 86, 90, 93, 103.

78 interacts with 3, 4, 16, 23, 34, 38, 45, 56, 58, 73, 79, 85, 86, 101, 105, 130.

79 interacts with 3, 4, 13, 16, 18, 23, 35, 38, 45, 71, 77, 78, 86, 88, 90, 104, 105, 111, 116, 124, 127, 130.

80 interacts with 7, 9, 12, 13, 17, 20, 31, 34, 36, 54, 55, 56, 86, 94, 103, 106, 123, 136.

81 interacts with 9, 12, 13, 17, 25, 27, 29, 36, 64, 82, 83, 85, 86, 92, 93, 113, 114, 119, 122, 133, 136.

82 interacts with 6, 16, 23, 24, 81, 111, 113, 115.

83 interacts with 13, 23, 77, 81, 85, 86, 101.

84 interacts with 20, 65, 120, 127, 131, 132, 134, 135.

85 interacts with 7, 12, 18, 26, 29, 48, 50, 56, 62, 64, 76, 78, 81, 83, 86, 87, 93, 108, 136.

86 interacts with 1, 3, 7, 12, 13, 14, 17, 19, 27, 36, 43, 48, 49, 56, 57, 61, 62, 63, 64, 67, 68, 70, 77, 78, 79, 80, 81, 83, 85, 103, 111, 117, 119, 120, 121, 123, 124, 125, 140, 141.

87 interacts with 12, 44, 50, 62, 76, 85, 90, 91, 93, 95, 100, 128.

88 interacts with 4, 16, 27, 29, 71, 79, 114, 123.

89 interacts with 8, 17, 20, 21, 31, 62, 100, 130, 138, 141.

90 interacts with 12, 25, 26, 27, 33, 34, 76, 77, 79, 87, 91, 93, 113, 114, 121, 124, 132.

91 interacts with 4, 12, 13, 26, 33, 34, 45, 52, 54, 60, 73, 76, 87, 90, 103, 105, 121, 132.

92 interacts with 25, 26, 27, 28, 29, 34, 41, 56, 67, 69, 76, 81, 114, 122, 123, 124, 132.

93 interacts with 10, 12, 23, 24, 26, 62, 63, 66, 77, 81, 87, 90, 116, 130, 132, 137, 141.

94 interacts with 13, 31, 34, 36, 38, 50, 54, 55, 57, 60, 68, 80, 103, 106, 119, 136.

95 interacts with 8, 11, 15, 16, 21, 23, 30, 61, 64, 76, 87, 102, 112, 117, 119, 121, 130, 132, 133, 135, 139, 141.

96 interacts with 8, 11, 15, 21, 58, 59, 61, 63, 97, 102, 119, 121, 130, 132, 133, 139, 141.

97 interacts with 14, 15, 18, 22, 30, 37, 38, 39, 40, 44, 48, 49, 60, 61, 96, 98, 119, 132, 133, 135.

98 interacts with 2, 15, 18, 22, 30, 31, 41, 44, 58, 59, 60, 61, 71, 75, 76, 97, 109, 110, 119, 120, 121, 132, 133, 139.

99 interacts with 8, 48, 58, 59, 61, 63, 64, 65, 131, 132, 133, 138.

100 interacts with 23, 24, 63, 64, 75, 87, 89, 101, 112, 113, 115, 121, 126, 130, 132, 133, 135, 141.

101 interacts with 1, 3, 9, 13, 16, 17, 23, 24, 29, 43, 64, 68, 76, 78, 83, 100, 102, 112, 113, 117, 119, 122, 133.

102 interacts with 2, 5, 6, 10, 20, 24, 56, 95, 96, 101, 115.

103 interacts with 3, 18, 28, 37, 50, 60, 77, 80, 86, 91, 94.

104 interacts with 19, 22, 32, 33, 35, 39, 40, 41, 42, 43, 45, 51, 52, 69, 70, 71, 72, 73, 75, 79, 105, 107, 109.

105 interacts with 2, 4, 7, 23, 32, 33, 34, 42, 45, 48, 61, 69, 71, 73, 74, 78, 79, 91, 104, 106, 110, 119, 137.

106 interacts with 1, 4, 7, 13, 19, 28, 31, 36, 38, 45, 46, 52, 54, 80, 94, 105, 129, 136.

107 interacts with 19, 22, 28, 30, 31, 32, 33, 34, 40, 41, 42, 43, 46, 47, 48, 49, 51, 52, 54, 69, 71, 74, 75, 104, 110, 122, 136.

108 interacts with 13, 24, 26, 28, 61, 73, 76, 85, 109, 110.

109 interacts with 28, 31, 32, 43, 48, 61, 64, 68, 71, 73, 74, 98, 104, 108, 110.

110 interacts with 4, 17, 18, 19, 22, 28, 32, 33, 36, 42, 43, 44, 45, 48, 49, 54, 61, 68, 70, 71, 73, 74, 98, 105, 107, 108, 109, 137.

111 interacts with 6, 8, 21, 25, 65, 79, 82, 86, 113, 115, 116, 117, 120, 130, 132, 134.

112 interacts with 8, 15, 21, 64, 95, 100, 101, 130, 133, 139, 141.

113 interacts with 1, 5, 9, 21, 26, 27, 64, 76, 81, 82, 90, 100, 101, 111, 114, 117, 119, 124.

114 interacts with 8, 11, 16, 25, 27, 62, 65, 68, 81, 88, 90, 92, 113, 117, 123, 127, 130, 132.

115 interacts with 8, 17, 21, 23, 24, 54, 62, 82, 100, 102, 111, 127, 132, 137, 140, 141.

116 interacts with 5, 8, 15, 17, 20, 21, 23, 25, 62, 63, 65, 79, 111, 117, 121, 127, 128, 131, 132, 135, 137.

117 interacts with 6, 16, 17, 20, 49, 57, 86, 95, 101, 111, 113, 114, 116, 121, 123, 124, 125, 133, 135, 137.

118 interacts with 5, 9, 17, 19, 28, 33, 34, 35, 39, 40, 41, 42, 45, 46, 47, 49, 51, 53, 57, 126, 127, 130, 131, 134.

119 interacts with 3, 16, 23, 29, 48, 55, 61, 62, 63, 68, 81, 86, 94, 95, 96, 97, 98, 101, 105, 113, 136.

120 interacts with 25, 61, 71, 76, 84, 86, 98, 111, 121, 126, 132, 133, 139.

121 interacts with 8, 12, 13, 14, 86, 90, 91, 95, 96, 98, 100, 116, 117, 120, 123, 124, 125, 127, 132, 133, 139.

122 interacts with 12, 13, 16, 26, 27, 29, 32, 33, 34, 41, 67, 76, 92, 101, 107, 123.

123 interacts with 2, 7, 26, 34, 55, 56, 57, 67, 75, 76, 80, 86, 88, 92, 114, 117, 121, 122, 127, 137.

124 interacts with 1, 4, 7, 9, 26, 29, 34, 55, 56, 68, 75, 76, 79, 86, 90, 92, 113, 117, 121, 137.

125 interacts with 7, 15, 40, 41, 45, 58, 59, 86, 117, 121.

126 interacts with 17, 19, 30, 33, 53, 57, 100, 118, 120, 133.

127 interacts with 15, 22, 28, 30, 33, 39, 40, 41, 45, 51, 53, 57, 58, 59, 61, 62, 63, 64, 65, 74, 76, 79, 84, 114, 115, 116, 118, 121, 123, 132, 135.

128 interacts with 15, 31, 33, 37, 38, 49, 72, 87, 116, 138, 140.

129 interacts with 8, 9, 12, 13, 14, 15, 17, 20, 28, 30, 32, 43, 48, 49, 63, 68, 71, 106, 131, 140.

130 interacts with 6, 10, 14, 15, 24, 26, 27, 30, 45, 46, 47, 48, 49, 58, 59, 62, 63, 64, 65, 66, 72, 78, 79, 89, 93, 95, 96, 100, 111, 112, 114, 118, 134, 137, 141.

131 interacts with 5, 20, 28, 30, 31, 60, 61, 68, 70, 71, 72, 84, 99, 116, 118, 129, 135.

132 interacts with 15, 23, 30, 31, 49, 62, 63, 66, 68, 69, 70, 71, 84, 90, 91, 92, 93, 95, 96, 97, 98, 99, 100, 111, 114, 115, 116, 120, 121, 127.

133 interacts with 2, 5, 10, 11, 14, 15, 20, 24, 30, 37, 49, 63, 64, 65, 66, 71, 75, 81, 95, 96, 97, 98, 99, 100, 101, 112, 117, 120, 121, 126, 134, 136, 139, 140.

134 interacts with 6, 10, 11, 33, 39, 40, 63, 65, 84, 111, 118, 130, 133.

135 interacts with 6, 15, 17, 24, 84, 95, 97, 100, 116, 117, 127, 131, 137.

136 interacts with 8, 9, 34, 36, 51, 52, 63, 64, 80, 81, 85, 94, 106, 107, 119, 133, 140.

137 interacts with 13, 15, 21, 23, 33, 35, 39, 40, 42, 53, 57, 66, 93, 105, 110, 115, 116, 117, 123, 124, 130, 135, 140.

138 interacts with 14, 15, 33, 39, 40, 41, 45, 49, 58, 59, 62, 63, 65, 89, 128, 140, 141.

139 interacts with 21, 30, 61, 64, 65, 66, 95, 96, 98, 112, 120, 121, 133.

140 interacts with 1, 5, 8, 9, 12, 13, 18, 19, 20, 21, 22, 24, 37, 43, 49, 61, 63, 86, 115, 128, 129, 133, 136, 137, 138, 141.

141 interacts with 1, 8, 9, 12, 13, 14, 15, 18, 21, 24, 48, 61, 62, 63, 65, 66, 68, 86, 89, 93, 95, 96, 100, 112, 115, 130, 138, 140.

Each link or absence of a link is a statement about the inter-action between the two variables concerned. If what we can do physically about meeting one requirement in the form inevitably affects what we can do about the other (whether positively or negatively), we call the variables linked. If there is no such inter-action, we call them independent.

Here is an example. Number 94 is the need for provision for animal traffic. This conflicts with 7, the need for cattle to be treated as sacred, because the sacredness of cattle allows the cattle great freedom, and hence more room for circulation, which makes 94 harder to meet adequately. On the other hand, 94 connects positively with 13, the need for family solidarity, because this latter requirement tends to group the houses of family members in compounds, and so reduces the number of access points required by cattle, making 94 easier to meet.

The complete list of interactions defines the set L. As we have seen before, the set M of misfit variables, together with the set L of links, define the graph $G(M,L)$.

Analysis of the graph $G(M,L)$, shows us the decomposition pic-tured below, where M itself falls into four major subsets A,B,C,D, and where these sets themselves break into twelve minor subsets, A1,A2,A3,B1,B2,B3,B4,C1,C2,D1,D2,D3, thus:

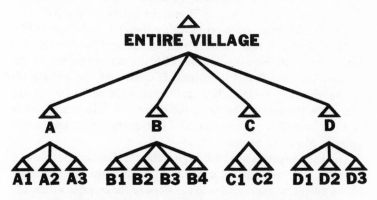

A1 contains requirements 7, 53, 57, 59, 60, 72, 125, 126, 128.
A2 contains requirements 31, 34, 36, 52, 54, 80, 94, 106, 136.
A3 contains requirements 37, 38, 50, 55, 77, 91, 103.
B1 contains requirements 39, 40, 41, 44, 51, 118, 127, 131, 138.
B2 contains requirements 30, 35, 46, 47, 61, 97, 98.

B3 contains requirements 18, 19, 22, 28, 33, 42, 43, 49, 69, 74, 107, 110.

B4 contains requirements 32, 45, 48, 70, 71, 73, 75, 104, 105, 108, 109.

C1 contains requirements 8, 10, 11, 14, 15, 58, 63, 64, 65, 66, 93, 95, 96, 99, 100, 112, 121, 130, 132, 133, 134, 139, 141.

C2 contains requirements 5, 6, 20, 21, 24, 84, 89, 102, 111, 115, 116, 117, 120, 129, 135, 137, 140.

D1 contains requirements 26, 29, 56, 67, 76, 85, 87, 90, 92, 122, 123, 124.

D2 contains requirements 1, 9, 12, 13, 25, 27, 62, 68, 81, 86, 113, 114.

D3 contains requirements 2, 3, 4, 16, 17, 23, 78, 79, 82, 83, 88, 101, 119.

The tree of diagrams made during the realization of this program is illustrated on the next page.

I first give a summary of the diagrams, and the way they fit together, so that the more detailed account of each diagram and the functions which belong to it may be better understood.

The four main diagrams are roughly these: A deals with cattle, bullock carts, and fuel; B deals with agricultural production, irrigation, and distribution; C deals with the communal life of the village, both social and industrial; D deals with the private life of the villagers, their shelter, and small-scale activities. Of the four, B is the largest, being of the order of a mile across, while A, C, D, are all more compact, and fit together in an area of the order of 200 yards across.

The basic organization of B is given by the diagram B4, a water collector unit, consisting of a high bund, built in the highest corner of the village, at right angles to the slope of the terrain; within the curve of this bund, water gullies run together in a tank. This tank serves the rest of the village land, which lies lower, by means of sluices in the bund; the component B4 is intimately connected with B3, the distribution system for the fields. The principal element of this diagram is a road elevated from floods, which naturally

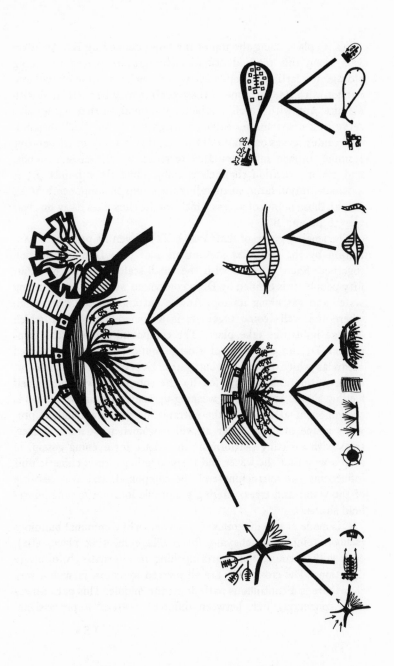

takes its place along the top of the bund defined by B4. At intervals along this road, distribution centers are placed providing storage for fertilizer, implements, and seeds; in view of the connection with B4, each one of these centers may be associated with a sluice, and with a well dug below the bund, so that it may also serve as a distribution center for irrigation water. Each distribution center serves one unit of type B2; this is a unit of cooperative farming, broken into contoured terraces, by anti-erosion bunds, and minor irrigation channels running along these bunds. B1 is a demonstration farm, surrounding the group of components ACD, just at those points of access which the farmers pass daily on their way to B2 and B3.

The smaller group of diagrams ACD is given its primary organization by the fact that several units of type D must function together. Each D copes with the small-scale activities of about fifty people. It is defined by D2, a compound wall carrying drinking water and gas along its top. At the entrance to the compound, where the walls come together, is a roofed area under which cottage industries take place. The compound contains the component D1, an assembly of storage huts, connected by roofed verandas which provide living space. Every third or fourth hut has a water tank on top, fed by the compound wall, and itself feeding simple bathing and washing-up spaces behind walls. D3 is a component attached to the entrance of the compound; it provides a line of open water at which women may wash clothes, trees with a sitting platform at their base for evening gossip, in such a way that the water and trees together form a climatic unit influencing the microclimate of the compound, and also, because of the water and trees, offering a suitable location for the household shrine.

C is made of two diagrams; C2 is a series of communal buildings (school, temple, panchayat office, village meeting place, etc.), each with a court, the courts opening in alternatingly opposite directions. The cross walls are all pierced by gates, in such a way that there is a continuous path down the middle. This path serves as a connecting link between different centers, a processional route, and pedestrian access to the compounds D which may there-fore be hung from C2 like a cluster of grapes. One end of this component C2 runs into C1; C1 is a widening of the road on the bund; on this widening out, a number of parallel walls are built to mark out narrow, city-like plots. There is in the center of these plots a bus stop, opening out of the road itself. The whole unit houses whatever industry, power sources, and other aspects of the village's future economic base, develop.

The structure of A starts with A2, a group of cattle stalls, each stall opening toward the outside only, its floor falling toward the center, with a drain in the center leading all manure to a pit where the slurry for the gober gas plant can be prepared. Each compound has such a component A2 in its center, between the pieces of D1; exit from the compound, for cattle and carts, is by way of component A3, a gate in the compound wall, marked by the cattle trough and the gober gas plant itself. A group of several components A2 and A3 are tied together by the single A1. A1 consists of a central control point through which all cattle leaving any compound have to pass. This control point provides a hoof bath, a dairy, and a link to the main road via C1.

During the actual realization of the program, that stage came last in which the four diagrams A, B, C, D, were combined to give the diagram labeled "Entire Village."

There now follows a more detailed account of the reasons behind the organization of each of the twelve minor diagrams.

A1: 7 Cattle treated as sacred and vegetarian attitude.
     53 Upgrading of cattle.
     57 Protection of cattle from disease.
     59 Efficient use and marketing of dairy products.
     60 Minimize the use of animal traction to take pressure off shortage.
     72 Prevent famine if monsoon fails.
    125 Prevent malnutrition.
    126 Close contact with village-level worker.
    128 Price assurance for crops.

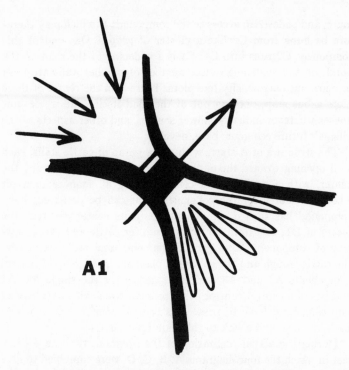

A1

The sacredness of cattle (7) tends to make people unwilling to control them, so they wander everywhere eating and destroying crops, unless they are carefully controlled. Similarly, the need to upgrade cattle (53) calls for a control which keeps cows out of contact with roaming scrub bulls; and further calls for some sort of center where a pedigree bull might be kept (even if only for visits); and a center where scrub bulls can be castrated. Cattle diseases (57) are mainly transferred from foot to foot, through the dirt — this can be prevented if the cattle regularly pass through a hoof bath of disinfecting permanganate. If milk (59) is to be sold cooperatively, provision must be made for central milking (besides processing); if cows are milked at home, and the milk then pooled, individual farmers will adulterate the milk. Famine prevention (72), the prevention of malnutrition (125), and price assurance for crops (128) all suggest some kind of center offering both storage, and production of nourishing foods (milk, eggs, groundnuts). If the village-level worker (126) is to come often to the village and help, quarters must be provided for him here. Animal traction (60) calls for access to and from the cattle stalls (A2) on the one hand, and the road on the other.

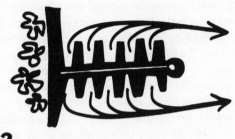

A2

A2: 31 Efficient distribution of fertilizer, manure, seed, from village storage to fields.
    34 Full collection of natural manure (animal and human).
    36 Protection of crops from thieves, cattle, goats, monkeys, etc.
    52 Improve quantity of fodder available.
    54 Provision for feeding cattle.
    80 Security for cattle.
    94 Provision for animal traffic.
  106 Young trees need protection from goats, etc.
  136 Accommodation of wandering caste groups, incoming labor, etc.

Here 31, 34, 54, 80, and 94 form a subset connected with cattle movement and manure, while 36, 52, 106, and 136 form a subset mainly concerned with the protection of crops and trees from wandering cattle. 31 and 34 call for the collection of urine and dung, which suggests cattle should be in one place as much of the time as possible, where there is a pucca floor draining toward a central manure collector. This is of course closely connected with feeding stalls, the most permanent standing place for cattle. 80 calls for psychological security — cattle owners want their cattle as near to them as possible, if not actually in the house, and are therefore absolutely opposed to the idea of a central communal cattle shed. In view of disease and germ-breeding difficulties the closest arrangement possible seems to be one where individual stalls are immediately opposite owners' verandas with nothing but a path between; this path serves to accommodate cattle traffic (94). Each stall is marked by its walls, roofed only by wood purlins at 2' centers, so that the fodder itself, stored on top, provides shade. Rains are not heavy enough to warrant permanent roofing. Vegetables, young trees, etc., which would be specially benefited by protection from cattle, must either be very far away, or else very close so that separation can really be achieved by a barrier (36, 106). To make this work, 52 must be assured by other means — stall feeding perhaps, which then connects with 54. To prevent the cattle of wandering shepherds from causing trouble (136), the proper grazing ground must abut the road, and access to it must be the normal road-village access. This grazing ground should be on the good land side of the bund, so that when green silage is introduced, land can be irrigated and cultivated.

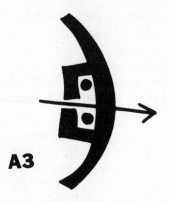

A3

A3: 37 Provision of storage for distributing and marketing crops.
38 Provision of threshing floor and its protection from marauders.
50 Protected storage of fodder.
55 Cattle access to water.
77 Village and individual houses must be protected from fire.
91 Provision and storage of fuel.
103 Bullock cart access to house for bulk of grain, fodder.

Access for cattle to water (55) should be to good water, hence to drinking water distribution system, feeding off compound wall D2. 77 and 91 are best achieved by a controlled fuel supply, like gas, supplied by a gober gas plant using manure from A2, the gas distributed to individual kitchens by the same artery that distributes water, i.e., the compound wall.

At the point on the compound wall indicated by these previous items, there must be an opening to allow passage of bullock carts (103), and at this point there should also be a store for supplies and fodder — or at least an easy unloading and access point to the roofs of the cattle bays (37, 38, 50).

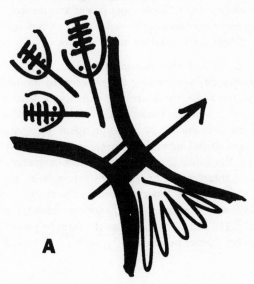

A

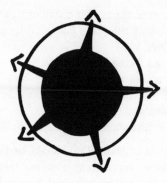

B1

B1: 39 Best cotton and cash crop.
  40 Best food grain crop.
  41 Good vegetable crop.
  44 Crops must be brought home from fields.
  51 Improve quality of fodder available.
  118 Demonstration projects which spread by example.
  127 Contact with block development officer.
  131 Panchayat must have more power and respect.
  138 Achieve economic independence so as not to strain national transportation and resources.

39, 40, 41, 51, and economic independence (138) are all items which can only be improved by the widespread use of improved agricultural methods; these are not directly dependent on the physical plan, but on a change of attitude in the villagers. This change of attitude cannot be brought about by sporadic visits from the agricultural extension officer and village-level worker, but only by the continuing presence of demonstration methods, on site (118); there should be a demonstration farm, government- or panchayat-owned (131), perhaps run by the village-level worker in association with the panchayat (hence accommodation for such officers, 127). 118 and 44 suggest that the farm be placed in such a way that every farmer passes it daily, on his way to and from the fields.

B2

B2: 30 Efficient and rapid distribution of seeds, fertilizer, etc., from block HQ.

35 Protection of crops from insects, weeds, disease.

46 Respect for traditional agricultural practices.

47 Need for new implements when old ones are damaged, etc.

61 Sufficient fluid employment for laborers temporarily (seasonally) out of work.

97 Minimize transportation costs for bulk produce (grain, potatoes, etc.).

98 Daily produce requires cheap and constant (monsoon) access to market.

97 and 98 are critical, and call for access to and from the fields on a road which is not closed in the monsoon — i.e., on an embankment. 30 and 35 call for efficient distribution within the plots, of seeds, fertilizers, insecticides, etc., which must themselves be stored at some point where delivery is easy — i.e., on the road. Hence the idea of distribution centers located at intervals along the main road, serving wedge-shaped or quasi-circular units of agricultural land. 46, 47, 61, have little discernible physical implication.

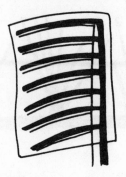

B3

B3: 18   Need to divide land among sons of successive generations.

  19   People want to own land personally.

  22   Abolition of Zamindari and uneven land distribution.

  28   Proper boundaries of ownership and maintenance responsibility.

  33   Fertile land to be used to best advantage.

  42   Efficient plowing, weeding, harvesting, leveling.

  43   Consolidation of land.

  49   Cooperative farming.

  69   Fullest possible irrigation benefit derived from available water.

  74   Maintenance of irrigation facilities.

107   Soil conservation.

110   Prevent land erosion.

18–49 all point to the development of cooperative farms of some sort, from the point of view of increasing efficiency of resources, manpower, machines, better crops, rotation of crops, etc. 69 cannot be implemented unless water is distributed from the HQ of such cooperatives because otherwise faction and personal rivalries, etc., prevent full use of wells — i.e., warring neighbors adjacent to the source of water (well) will not agree to cooperate about sharing its use. Irrigation (74) requires consolidated ownership of channels, otherwise neglect at one place holds up the efficient use somewhere else. Soil conservation (107) depends on rotation of crops, which is only feasible if large plots are under single ownership control, so that they can carry the full pattern of rotation. Erosion (110) is prevented by long continuous contour bunds, which can only be put across land of integrated ownership. Bund and irrigation divisions on contours suggest terraced strips of land as units of co-op farm, fed from single uphill source.

B4

B4: 32   Reclamation and use of uncultivated land.

   45   Development of horticulture.

   48   Scarcity of land.

   70   Full collection of underground water for irrigation.

   71   Full collection of monsoon water for use.

   73   Conservation of water resources for future.

   75   Drainage of land to prevent waterlogging, etc.

  104   Plant ecology to be kept healthy.

  105   Insufficient forest land.

  108   Road and dwelling erosion.

  109   Reclamation of eroded land, gullies, etc.

32 and 48 call for use of wasteland, which often contains river bed area. 48 calls for irrigation of this area. 71, 73, 75, suggest the use of monsoon water instead of and as well as well water for irrigation, since well irrigation is temporary in the long run, because it causes a drop in the water table. Apart from actually using monsoon water for irrigation, the water table in the wells can be preserved if the wells are backed up by a tank. Hence a curved bund collects water above wells placed under the bund (70). Rainfall in the catchment area (again a water resource issue, 73) will be improved by tree planting (104, 105), which suggests putting fruit trees (45) inside the curve of the bund. (Incidentally, placing the trees within the bund offers us a way of protecting young trees from cattle, by keeping the cattle on the other side of the bund, which then forms a natural barrier.) Further, if water is to flow toward the tank, horizontal contour bunds cannot be used to check erosion as they are in B3, so erosion of gullies, streams, etc., can only be controlled by tree planting (109). Road erosion is controlled if the road is on top of the bund itself (108).

B

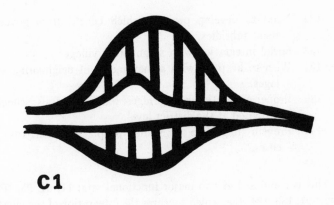

C1

C1:   8   Members of castes maintain their caste profession as far as possible.
      10 Need for elaborate weddings.
      11 Marriage is to person from another village.
      14 Economic integration of village on payment-in-kind basis.
      15 Modern move toward payment in cash.
      58 Development of other animal industry.
      63 Development of village industry.
      64 Simplify the mobility of labor, to and from villages, and to and from fields and industries and houses.
      65 Diversification of village's economic base — not all occupations agricultural.
      66 Efficient provision and use of power.
      93 Lighting.
      95 Access to bus as near as possible.
      96 Access to railway station.
      99 Industry requires strong transportation support.
      100 Provision for bicycle age in every village by 1965.
      112 Access to a secondary school.
      121 Facilities for birth, pre- and post-natal care (birth control).
      130 Need for increased incentives and aspirations.

132 Need to develop projects which benefit from government subsidies.
133 Social integration with neighboring villages.
134 Wish to keep up with achievements of neighboring villages.
139 Proper connection with bridges, roads, hospitals, schools, proposed at the district level.
141 Prevent migration of young people and harijans to cities.

This is composed of two major functional sets: 11, 64, 95, 100, 112, 121, 133, 134, 139, which concerns the integration of the village with neighboring villages and with the region, and 8, 10, 14, 15, 58, 63, 65, 66, 93, 96, 99, 130, 132, 141, which concerns the future economic base of the village, and all the aspects of "modern" life and society.

These two are almost inseparable. They call for a center, away from the heart of the village, on the road, able, because of being on the road, to sustain connections between the village and other villages (11) and capable of acting as a meeting place for villagers of different villages (112, 121). This function is promoted by the need to provide a bus stop (95), village industries with optimum access to the road (63–66, 99), the social gathering place connected with the bus and with jobs made available by the industries (61, 133, 134); the development of a modern and almost urban atmosphere to combat migration of the best people to cities (141), and to develop incentives (14, 15, 130, 132). A center of industry promotes 8, 63, 64. The road satisfies 64, 95, 96, 99, 100, 139. The center will be the natural physical location for sources of power and electricity transformer (66, 93); also the most efficient place for the poultry and dairy farming which require road access (58); the bus stop is the natural arrival place for incoming wedding processions (10).

C2

The major fact about the communal social life of the village is the presence of factions, political parties, etc.; these can be a great hindrance to development (20, 129). If the various communal facilities of the village (5, 6, 24, 84, 89, 111, 115, 120, 137) are provided in a central place, this place will very likely get associated with one party, or certain families, and may actually not contribute to social life at all. On the other hand, it is important from the point of view of social integration (21, 140) to provide a single structure rather than isolated buildings. What is more, isolated buildings also have the possible connection with the single family nearest them, which can again discourage other families from going there. What is required is a community center which somehow manages to pull all the communal functions together so that none are left isolated, but at the same time does not have a location more in favor of some families than others. To achieve this, a linear center, containing some buildings facing in, some out, zigzagging between the different compounds, is necessary. This also meets (102) the need for processions with important stopping places; and adult literacy calls for a series of walls along the major pedestrian paths, with the alphabet and messages written in such a way that their continuing presence forces people to absorb them (116, 117, 135).

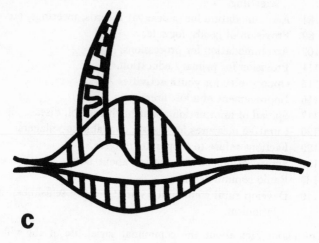

c

D1

D1: 26   Sentimental system: wish not to destroy old way of life; love of present habits governing bathing, food, etc.

    29   Provision for daily bath, segregated by sex, caste, and age.

    56   Sheltered accommodation for cattle (sleeping, milking, feeding).

    67   Drinking water to be good, sweet.

    76   Flood control to protect houses, roads, etc.

    85   Everyone's accommodation for sitting and sleeping should be protected from rain.

    87   Safe storage of goods.

    90   Better provision for preparing meals.

    92   House has to be cleaned, washed, drained.

  122   Disposal of human excreta.

  123   Prevent breeding germs and disease starters.

  124   Prevent spread of human disease by carriers, infection, contagion.

Houses, as they are used at present, are chiefly storerooms; people actually live on their verandas most of the time. The one thing which inner rooms provide, namely privacy and psychological security, appears among the needs to be met by D2, not here. Hence, we solve 87 by providing storerooms, which in a column-like manner support veranda roofs stretching between them (85). 26 is mainly concerned with bathing and food, connected with (29, 67, 90). These suggest a water store on top of occasional storehouses, with kitchen and bath wall attached to this store (also 122); probably this water store will be fairly close to the source of water, as we shall see when we combine this with D2. The floor of the veranda must be raised to keep it out of flood water (76) — also the compound should drain toward the center, to remove the dangers of 92, 123, 124. 56 calls for a space to house A2.

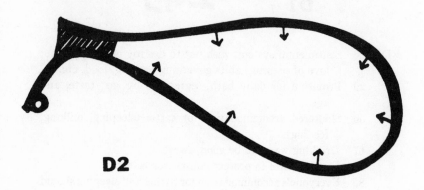

D2

D2: 1 Harijans regarded as ritually impure, untouchable, etc.
9 Members of one caste like to be together and separate from others, and will not eat or drink together.
12 Extended family is in one house.
13 Family solidarity and neighborliness even after separation.
25 Assistance for physically handicapped, aged, widows.
27 Family is authoritarian.
62 Provision of cottage industry and artisan workshops and training.
68 Easy access to drinking water.
81 Security for women and children.
86 No overcrowding.
113 Good attendance in school.
114 Development of women's independent activities.

1, 9, 12, 13, suggest group compounds, as they are found at present, each of about 5 to 10 families, i.e., 25 to 50 persons. To provide security (81), especially for women, surround it by a wall, whose top serves as a distribution channel for water (68). The fact that the space within the wall is all protected, allows women more freedom within the compound for women's communal activities (114), gives more freedom to widows (25), and allows cottage industries, which are likely to be run largely by women, to flourish (62). The space for cottage industry (62) should go at the entrance to the compound, where women going to and from washing activities pass it constantly; this may to some extent combat the effects of purdah (27); it encourages women to come out from their houses (which the usual house discourages, because it allows women to shut themselves up in seclusion), and may even help girls' attendance in school by making the women more bold (113). Since containing walls are moved outward, overcrowding is less likely to take place (86) — adjustment and expansion can take place more easily within the compound walls than within individual house walls.

D3

D3: 2 Proper disposal of dead.
    3 Rules about house door not facing south.
    4 Certain water and certain trees are thought of as sacred.

16 Women gossip extensively while bathing, fetching water, on way to field latrines, etc.

17 Village has fixed men's social groups.

23 Men's groups chatting, smoking, even late at night.

78 Shade for sitting and walking.

79 Provision of cool breeze.

82 Provision for children to play (under supervision).

83 In summer people sleep in open.

88 Place to wash and dry clothes.

101 Pedestrian traffic within village.

119 Efficient use of school; no distraction of students.

Here there are several overlapping functions. 23, 78, 79, 82, 83, all require the control of climate — in particular getting cool conditions — which can be best achieved by the juxtaposition of water and trees. 16, 17, 23, 88, 101, require a unit for gossip, washing clothes, meeting purposes, at the compound level. 2, 3, 4, demand the construction of a place with certain qualities of sacredness, perhaps quiet, water, neem trees. Pedestrian traffic and quiet are called for again by 101, 119. All these functions call for a unit in which water, trees, washing facilities, pedestrian movement, sitting under the trees, are juxtaposed; the unit fits directly onto the compound, just outside the entrance. Washing may be either on ghats, etc., or on steps fed from the water wall unit D2.

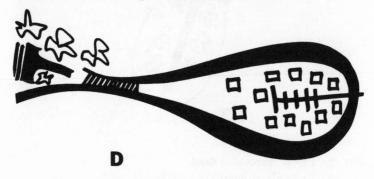

D

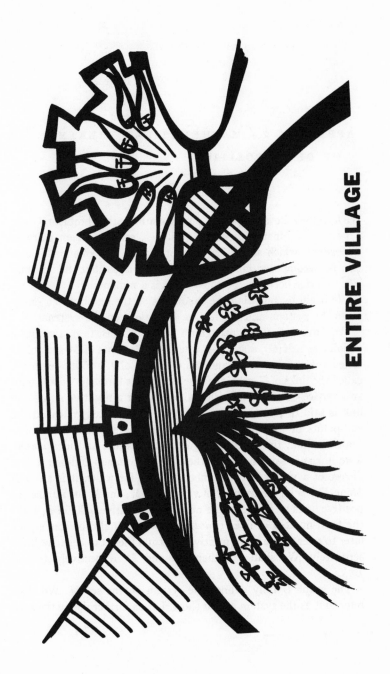

ENTIRE VILLAGE

We face the following specific, purely mathematical problem. Given a system of binary stochastic variables, some of them pairwise dependent, which satisfy certain conditions, how should this system be decomposed into a set of subsystems, so that the information transfer between the subsystems is a minimum?

We begin by restating the conditions on the graph which represents the system, and the further conditions on the system.

We have a finite signed graph G which consists of two finite disjoint sets $M(G)$, and $L(G)$, where the elements of M are points called the vertices of G, and the elements of L are line-segments called the links of G, each one of which passes through two and only two vertices, and carries either a positive or a negative sign.[1] The link is said to join these two vertices. The vertices are called the end-points of the link. Where two vertices are joined by more than one link, the links are regarded as distinct and identifiable. Two links are said to meet if they have a common end-point. The degree of a vertex is the number of links for which it is an end-point. Let m be the number of vertices in M, and l^+ the number of positive links in L, and l^- the number of negative links in L, and l the total number of links ($l = l^+ + l^-$). It will also be convenient later to refer to the set of positive links and the set of negative links separately. We shall call them L^+ and L^- respectively (where $L^+ \cup L^- = L$).

The graph G fully defines the system on the set M. We shall refer to it as the system M, for short. Let us further define the subsystems of M as follows. Given any subset of S of M, construct that graph whose vertices are the points of S, and whose links are just those elements of L for which both end-points belong to S. We call such a graph a full subgraph of G. It is clear that once L is given, each subset S of M has a uniquely defined associated full subgraph of G. It fully defines a subsystem on S, which we may again call S for short.

Associated with the ith vertex of G is a binary random variable x_i, taking the values 0 and 1 with respective probabilities p and $1 - p$ (p being the same for all variables). We must at this point insert a brief note about this p. It is possible in practice that there might be a different p_i for each variable. However, it is clear that the decomposition of the system into subsystems cannot be invariant for any pattern of p_i's. In other words, if variable x_1 has a large probability of being 0, but all the other variables have a large probability of being 1, we cannot expect to get the same decomposition into subsystems as in the case where these probabilities are relatively very different.

If we allowed the p_i to be different for different variables x_i, we should have to bring this into the following analysis, which would lead to very complicated equations, and make it impossible to find a simple and general basis for decomposition. It is for this reason, to avoid an intolerably difficult mathematical problem, that we have arranged, as described in Chapter 8, to make all the variables in M have roughly equal scope or significance. And we write $p_i = p$ for all p_i, so that $p(x_i = 0) = p$ for all i, and $p(x_i = 1) = 1 - p$, for all i.

We shall now make a further assumption, to simplify the mathematics still further. The decomposition of M depends on the relative amounts of information transmitted from one subsystem to another. While the absolute amounts of information must of course depend on the absolute values of the state probabilities, the relative amounts should depend only on the relative values of state probabilities. We should expect, therefore, that the decomposition of the system into subsystems should be the same, no matter what the absolute value of p. In other words, on grounds of symmetry alone, it would be very strange if, by changing the probability p to some new value p^* for all variables simultaneously, we could alter the system's subsystems. We shall not try to prove this intuition. The reader is invited to reconsider it after reading the proof which follows. We shall assume that it is so, and that we may therefore base our decomposition on the most convenient possible value for p. The value we choose, for convenience of computation, is the one which satisfies $p = 1 - p$; i.e., $p = \frac{1}{2}$.

We therefore redefine the system, for the purpose of computation, so that there is, associated with the ith vertex of G, a binary stochastic variable x_i, taking the values 0 and 1 with *equal* probabilities, and we write $p(x_i = 0) = p(x_i = 1) = \frac{1}{2}$ for all x_i.

Since there are m variables in M, there are clearly 2^m ways of assigning them values. Each of these 2^m ways is called a state of the system M. (From an abstract point of view, we may also think of each vertex of the set M as being in one of two conditions, black or white, say, in which case we refer to the states of the system conveniently as colorings of the set M.) Each state of the m-variable system is completely defined by a row of m 1's and 0's (in the lexicographic order of the variables); we may call it σ for short. And similarly the state of any s-variable subsystem is defined by a row of s 1's and 0's, which we shall call λ for short.

In what follows we shall associate with each system a probability distribution over its states. We shall adopt the natural notation that $p(01100 \ldots)$, for instance, is the probability of the state defined by the row of 1's and 0's in the bracket. For the extreme case of a one-variable system, we have, as observed above, $p(0) = p(1) = \frac{1}{2}$ for all variables. If there is ever any ambiguity about which variables are referred to, we shall label the 1's and 0's with subscripts. Thus $p(0_j)$ is, specifically, the probability of x_j taking the value 0.

Consider M, or any of its subsystems S. Since each separate variable takes the values 0 and 1 with equal probability, then if the variables were all independent of one another, the 2^m states of M would be equiprobable, and for any S its 2^s states would be equiprobable. We should have:

$$p(\sigma) = \frac{1}{2^m} \text{ for all } \sigma, \text{ and } p(\lambda) = \frac{1}{2^s} \text{ for all } \lambda.$$

In general, however, since there is some kind of interaction between the variables, represented by the links, the various states of a system will not be equiprobable; and we face the problem of determining the $p(\sigma)$ or $p(\lambda)$ for different σ and λ. What are the conditions these distributions must satisfy?

Condition 1

The two-variable product moment correlation for each pair of variables (x_i, x_j) is $\nu_{ij}\delta$, where $\nu_{ij} = (|l_{ij}^+| - |l_{ij}^-|)$ is the signed number of links between the vertices i and j of G, and where δ is a constant, satisfying $l\delta \leqslant 1$. Since at most one of l_{ij}^+, l_{ij}^- is non zero, this makes ν_{ij} an integer lying between $-\nu$ and $+\nu$. It means also, that each individual link makes an equal contribution of δ to the correlation, positive or negative according to its sign. We get from this,[2] the fact that in every two-variable system (x_i, x_j), the $p(\lambda)$ must satisfy

$$\frac{p(00)p(11) - p(01)p(10)}{[p(0_i)p(1_i)p(0_j)p(1_j)]^{\frac{1}{2}}} = \nu_{ij}\delta.$$

Condition 2

We also know from Chapter 8 that all three variable and higher correlations vanish. What this means is that the value of the correlation function for any pair of variables is not dependent on the state of any other variable or set of variables in M,[3] i.e., formally we write

$$\frac{p(00\lambda)p(11\lambda) - p(01\lambda)p(10\lambda)}{[p(0_i\lambda)p(1_i\lambda)p(0_j\lambda)p(1_j\lambda)]^{\frac{1}{2}}} = \nu_{ij}\delta,$$

where λ represents any fixed pattern of values taken by any set of variables which does not include x_i and x_j. The simplest case, where λ is the state of a single variable x_k, say $x_k = 0$, gives the condition:

$$\frac{p(000_k)p(110_k) - p(010_k)p(100_k)}{[p(0_i0_k)p(1_i0_k)p(0_j0_k)p(1_j0_k)]^{\frac{1}{2}}} = \nu_{ij}\delta.$$

Among m variables, there are $\frac{1}{2}m(m-1) \cdot 3^{m-2}$ such conditions to be met, of which $2^m - (m+1)$ are independent.[4]

We now show that all the probability distributions for all subsystems are uniquely determined by the conditions stated, when we introduce the following further conditions which must be satisfied, by definition, by any probability distribution.

Condition 3

In any state of M, each of the m variables takes a fixed value. Take any subsystem S. Suppose, without loss of generality, we renumber the variables so that $x_1 \cdots x_s$ are in S, and $x_{s+1} \cdots x_m$ are not in S. Then in any state λ of S, each of the s variables $x_1 \cdots x_s$ takes a fixed value, and the remaining variables $x_{s+1} \cdots x_m$ are free. There are 2^{m-s} states of M in which the variables $x_1 \cdots x_s$ take the fixed pattern of values λ, one for each possible pattern of values taken by the set of $m-s$ free variables $x_{s+1} \cdots x_m$. We may therefore write the probability of λ as the sum of the probabilities of these 2^{m-s} states of M, thus:[5] $p(\lambda) = \sum p(\sigma)$ summed over all combinations of values for variables not in S.

Condition 4

Finally, we must have $p(\sigma) \geqslant 0$ for all σ.[6]

Condition 5

And we must have $\sum_{\sigma} p(\sigma) = 1$.[7]

We may use these facts as a way of building up the probabilities of the larger systems' states from the smaller, as follows.

Let us begin by considering the states of the 1-variable subsystems. We know by postulate, of course, that these probabilities $p(0)$ and $p(1)$ are $\frac{1}{2}$ and $\frac{1}{2}$. Let us now consider any 2-variable subsystem. We know 4 equations of the form: $p(00) + p(01) = p(0)$, of which 3 are independent, and we have 1 further equation from the fact that the graph G tells us the value of the correlation coefficient:

$$\frac{p(00)p(11) - p(01)p(10)}{[p(0)p(1)p(0)p(1)]^{\frac{1}{2}}}.$$

178

The probabilities of the 2-variable subsystem's states are therefore determinate.

Let us now consider any 3-variable subsystem. Again its state probabilities are determined to within one degree of freedom, by the probabilities of the constituent 2-variable subsystems' states, which we know. As before, the one degree of freedom is resolved by the fact that we know the value taken by one of the partial correlation functions of the form:

$$\frac{p(000)p(110) - p(010)p(100)}{[p(00)p(10)p(00)p(10)]^{\frac{1}{2}}}.$$

We thus see easily that at each stage of this process, the probabilities of the states of an s-variable subsystem, are determined to within 1 degree of freedom, by its constituent $(s - 1)$-variable-subsystems' state probabilities. And we can supply the one further constraint required to determine the probabilities uniquely, by looking at the appropriate partial correlation, whose value we know:

$$\frac{p(00\lambda)p(11\lambda) - p(01\lambda)p(10\lambda)}{[p(0\lambda)p(1\lambda)p(0\lambda)p(1\lambda)]^{\frac{1}{2}}},$$

where λ refers to some fixed state of $s - 2$ variables.

We shall now define a probability distribution which meets conditions 1–5, and must therefore be the unique distribution whose construction we have just described.[8]

In the state σ, call the links of L^+ satisfied or dissatisfied according as their end-points take the same or different values, and call the links of L^- satisfied or dissatisfied according as their end-points take different values or the same values. Then define the following:

$$e_{\sigma i} = +1 \text{ if vertex } x_i \text{ is 0 in state } \sigma,$$
$$e_{\sigma i} = -1 \text{ if vertex } x_i \text{ is 1 in state } \sigma,$$

so that $e_{\sigma i}e_{\sigma j}$ is 1 if the link ij is satisfied in σ,

and -1 if the link ij is dissatisfied in σ.

Then we define $\quad k_\sigma = \sum_{ij} v_{ij}e_{\sigma i}e_{\sigma j} \quad (i = 1 \cdots m, j = 1 \cdots m).$

In other words, the integer k_σ is the number of satisfied links in σ, less the number of dissatisfied links in σ. Hence, for all σ, $-l \leqslant k_\sigma \leqslant l$. Let us now consider the measure

$$p(\sigma) = \frac{1 + k_\sigma \delta}{2^m}.$$

Take condition 4 first:

We know that $\qquad\qquad k_\sigma \geqslant -l$.

Hence $\qquad\qquad p(\sigma) \geqslant \dfrac{1 - l\delta}{2^m}.$

Therefore $p(\sigma) \geqslant 0$ provided that $\delta < 1/l$, and this is so by postulate.[9]

Take next condition 5.

$$\sum_\sigma p(\sigma) = \sum_\sigma \frac{1 + k_\sigma \delta}{2^m} = 1 + \frac{\delta}{2^m} \sum_\sigma k_\sigma = 1 + \frac{\delta}{2^m} \sum_{ij} \nu_{ij} \sum_\sigma e_{\sigma i} e_{\sigma j}.$$

Now, if i and j are different, then in 2^{m-1} cases $e_{\sigma i}$ and $e_{\sigma j}$ will take the same sign so that their product is $+1$, and in 2^{m-1} cases they will take different signs so that their product is -1. Thus, for i and j different, the sum over all 2^m possible σ, vanishes. For i and j the same, ν_{ij} vanishes. Hence the last right hand side term is identical to 0.

$$\therefore \quad \sum_\sigma p(\sigma) = 1.$$

We next prove condition 3, namely that if the measure is defined for all subsystems S in the same way as it is for M, then all the relations of the form $p(\lambda) = \sum\limits_{\substack{\text{variables} \\ \text{not in } S}} p(\sigma)$ hold identically.

Since we get any subset S of M, by removing $m - s$ variables from M, one at a time, it is sufficient to prove the result for a single step of removing one variable, and the general result follows by induction. Consider, therefore, any variable x_k of M, and define S as the subsystem obtained from M by removing x_k. Pick an arbitrary λ of this subsystem S. Suppose σ_1 and σ_2 are the two states of M in which the variables of S are in the same condition as in λ, and for which x_k takes the value 0 in σ_1 and the value 1 in σ_2.

We wish to prove that $p(\sigma_1) + p(\sigma_2) = p(\lambda)$.
To see that this is so we note that

$$[p(\sigma_1) + p(\sigma_2)] - [p(\lambda)] = \frac{1 + k_{\sigma_1}\delta}{2^m} + \frac{1 + k_{\sigma_2}\delta}{2^m} - \frac{1 + k_\lambda\delta}{2^{m-1}}$$

$$= \frac{\delta}{2^m}\left(\sum_{ij} \nu_{ij}e_{\sigma_1 i}e_{\sigma_1 j} + \sum_{ij} \nu_{ij}e_{\sigma_2 i}e_{\sigma_2 j} - 2\sum_{ij} \nu_{ij}e_{\lambda i}e_{\lambda j}\right).$$

For $i, j \neq k$, $e_{\sigma_1 i}$, $e_{\sigma_2 i}$ and $e_{\lambda i}$ are identical. For i or $j = k$, the terms from σ_1 cancel with those from σ_2, which makes the right-hand side equal to 0, and proves the point.

We now return to the correlation coefficients. Let us first take the total correlation for a pair of variables, i and j. The above result allows us to write the state probabilities of the two variable subsystem, (x_i, x_j), as:

$$p(00) = \frac{1 + \nu_{ij}\delta}{4} \qquad\qquad p(10) = \frac{1 - \nu_{ij}\delta}{4}$$

$$p(01) = \frac{1 - \nu_{ij}\delta}{4} \qquad\qquad p(11) = \frac{1 + \nu_{ij}\delta}{4}$$

where ν_{ij} is the number of links between x_i and x_j in G. This gives a product moment correlation coefficient

$$\frac{p(00)p(11) - p(01)p(10)}{[p(0)p(1)p(0)p(1)]^{\frac{1}{2}}} = \frac{4\nu_{ij}\delta}{16}\Big/\frac{1}{4} = \nu_{ij}\delta,$$

and thus satisfies condition 1.

Consider finally, the partial correlation coefficient for any two variables x_i, x_j in any subsystem $(S + x_i + x_j)$ while the variables of S are held constant.

Let us picture this situation as below:

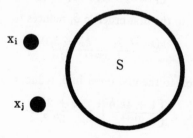

Suppose the variables in S are held constant in some fixed state λ, we may then write

$$p(00\lambda) = \frac{1 + (k_{00} + k_\lambda + k_i + k_j)\delta}{2^{s+2}},$$

where k_{00} is the term coming from the links between x_i and x_j, k_λ is the term coming from the links inside S, and k_i and k_j are the terms coming from the links between S and x_i, x_j, respectively. It is then easy to see that similarly

$$p(11\lambda) = \frac{1 + (k_{11} + k_\lambda - k_i - k_j)\delta}{2^{s+2}},$$

$$p(01\lambda) = \frac{1 + (k_{01} + k_\lambda + k_i - k_j)\delta}{2^{s+2}},$$

$$p(10\lambda) = \frac{1 + (k_{10} + k_\lambda - k_i + k_j)\delta}{2^{s+2}}.$$

Also

$$p(0_i\lambda) = \frac{1 + (k_\lambda + k_i)\delta}{2^{s+1}},$$

$$p(1_i\lambda) = \frac{1 + (k_\lambda - k_i)\delta}{2^{s+1}},$$

$$p(0_j\lambda) = \frac{1 + (k_\lambda + k_j)\delta}{2^{s+1}},$$

$$p(1_j\lambda) = \frac{1 + (k_\lambda - k_j)\delta}{2^{s+1}}.$$

The partial correlation is given by

$$\frac{p(00\lambda)p(11\lambda) - p(01\lambda)p(10\lambda)}{[p(0\lambda)p(1\lambda)p(0\lambda)p(1\lambda)]^{\frac{1}{2}}}.$$

The numerator, to the first order in δ, reduces to

$$\frac{(k_{00} + k_{11} - k_{01} - k_{10})\delta}{2^{2s+4}}.$$

The denominator, to the first order in δ, reduces to

$$\left[\frac{1 + 4k_\lambda\delta}{2^{4s+4}}\right]^{\frac{1}{2}} = \frac{1 + 2k_\lambda\delta}{2^{2s+2}}.$$

Since $\quad k_{00} = k_{11} = \nu_{ij} \quad$ and $\quad k_{01} = k_{10} = -\nu_{ij}$,

this makes the partial correlation equal to

$$\frac{4\nu_{ij}\delta}{4(1 + 2k_\lambda\delta)} = \nu_{ij}\delta$$

to the first order in δ, which is very small. Hence the partial correlation is $\nu_{ij}\delta$ for all λ, and satisfies condition 2.

Thus the measure

$$p(\sigma) = \frac{1 + k_\sigma\delta}{2^m}$$

has been shown to satisfy conditions 1–5, and is therefore, to within the stated approximations, that distribution uniquely determined by these conditions.

The probability distribution generated by this function for a specific graph is illustrated below.

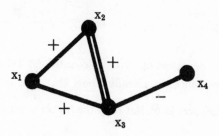

$$p(0000) = \frac{1 + 3\delta}{16} \qquad p(0011) = \frac{1 - 3\delta}{16} \qquad p(0111) = \frac{1 - \delta}{16}$$

$$p(0001) = \frac{1 + 5\delta}{16} \qquad p(0101) = \frac{1 - \delta}{16} \qquad p(1011) = \frac{1 - 3\delta}{16}$$

$$p(0010) = \frac{1 - \delta}{16} \qquad p(1001) = \frac{1 + \delta}{16} \qquad p(1101) = \frac{1 - \delta}{16}$$

$$p(0100) = \frac{1 - 3\delta}{16} \qquad p(0110) = \frac{1 + \delta}{16} \qquad p(1110) = \frac{1 + 5\delta}{16}$$

$$p(1000) = \frac{1 - \delta}{16} \qquad p(1010) = \frac{1 - \delta}{16} \qquad p(1111) = \frac{1 + 3\delta}{16}$$

$$p(1100) = \frac{1 - 3\delta}{16}$$

Since we now have a workable probability distribution defined over the states of M, we can write down an expression for the average information carried by the system M. We use the Shannon-Wiener measure, and define $H(M)$, the average information carried by M, as

$$- \sum_\sigma p(\sigma) \log p(\sigma).^{10}$$

We may rewrite this now, as

$$
\begin{aligned}
H(M) &= - \sum_\sigma \left(\frac{1 + k_\sigma \delta}{2^m} \right) \log \left(\frac{1 + k_\sigma \delta}{2^m} \right) \\
&= - \frac{1}{2^m} \sum_\sigma \{ (1 + k_\sigma \delta)[\log (1 + k_\sigma \delta) - m \log 2] \} \\
&= - \frac{1}{2^m} \sum_\sigma \left\{ (1 + k_\sigma \delta)(+ k_\sigma \delta - \frac{k_\sigma^2 \delta^2}{2} + \cdots - m \log 2) \right\} \\
&= - \frac{1}{2^m} \sum_\sigma \left\{ -m \log 2 + (1 - m \log 2) k_\sigma \delta + \frac{k_\sigma^2 \delta^2}{2} + \begin{matrix} \text{terms in } \delta^3 \\ \text{and above} \end{matrix} \right\}.
\end{aligned}
$$

In the sum, the constant term is counted 2^m times. The term in δ vanishes, since we already know that $\sum_\sigma k_\sigma = 0$. We therefore retain the term in δ^2, but drop the higher order terms, leaving

$$H(M) = m \log 2 - \frac{\delta^2}{2^{m+1}} \sum_\sigma k_\sigma^2.$$

Similarly we obtain, for any S,

$$H(S) = s \log 2 - \frac{\delta^2}{2^{s+1}} \sum_\lambda k_\lambda^2.$$

Even now, this expression for $H(S)$ is computationally impracticable. To compute it directly we should first have to compute the index k_λ for each of the 2^s states of the set S, as described above. For large s, even a high speed electronic computer will not be able to calculate and sum the powers of the 2^s values of k_λ in any reasonable time. It is therefore necessary, for computational purposes, to express $\sum_{\lambda} k_{\lambda}^2$ as a function of simpler structural parameters of the graph $G(S,L)$.

For the sake of notational simplicity, let us continue to work with the graph $G(M,L)$ and the function $\sum_{\sigma} k_{\sigma}^2$; by keeping the argument general, we may then again apply it to any of its subgraphs $G(S,L)$ and their associated functions $\sum_{\lambda} k_{\lambda}^2$.

We have defined $\qquad k_{\sigma} = \sum_{ij \epsilon L} v_{ij} e_{\sigma i} e_{\sigma j}.$

Since we specified earlier that where there are several links between a pair of vertices these links are individually identifiable, we may now rewrite this expression as

$$k_{\sigma} = \Big(\sum_{L^+} e_{\sigma i} e_{\sigma j} - \sum_{L^-} e_{\sigma i} e_{\sigma j}\Big),$$

where each sum is taken over all the links belonging to L^+ and L^- respectively, so that the total contains l terms. It must be understood, of course, that this expression could be reduced, since each of its l terms is either 1 or -1. But, for the sake of clarity in the following proof, we shall leave it in its expanded form. We may write, then,

$$\sum_{\sigma} (k_{\sigma})^2 = \sum_{\sigma} \Big(\sum_{L^+} e_{\sigma i} e_{\sigma j} - \sum_{L^-} e_{\sigma i} e_{\sigma j}\Big)^2$$
$$= \sum_{\sigma} \Big\{ \Big(\sum_{L^+} e_{\sigma i} e_{\sigma j}\Big)^2 + \Big(\sum_{L^-} e_{\sigma i} e_{\sigma j}\Big)^2 - 2\Big(\sum_{L^+} e_{\sigma i} e_{\sigma j} \sum_{L^-} e_{\sigma k} e_{\sigma l}\Big) \Big\}.$$

Let us first look at the last bracket in this expansion. Since no vertex pair can be connected by a link from L^+ and a link from L^- simultaneously, every term in this last bracket will be of the form $e_{\sigma i} e_{\sigma j}^2 e_{\sigma k}$ or of the form $e_{\sigma i} e_{\sigma j} e_{\sigma k} e_{\sigma l}$, i,j,k,l all different. Since $e_{\sigma i}$, for any given i, takes the value $+1$ for half the σ, and -1 for the other half of the σ, and is evenly distributed over the values taken by the $e_{\sigma j}$, $e_{\sigma k}$, and $e_{\sigma l}$, we see that either of the above forms, since they both contain an $e_{\sigma i}$ raised to an odd power, will vanish when summed over σ. Let us now look at the first and second brackets in their expanded form. Again, all terms of the form $e_{\sigma i} e_{\sigma j}{}^2 e_{\sigma k}$ or $e_{\sigma i} e_{\sigma j} e_{\sigma k} e_{\sigma l}$ will vanish when summed over σ. There are therefore only two kinds of term left, both of the form $e_{\sigma i}{}^2 e_{\sigma j}{}^2$: those which represent the same link taken twice, and those which represent different links between the same vertex pair. We are therefore left with

$$\sum_\sigma k_\sigma{}^2 = \sum_\sigma \sum_{\substack{\text{links } ij \text{ of} \\ \text{either } L^+ \text{ or} \\ L^- \text{ alone}}} (e_{\sigma i} e_{\sigma j})^2 + 2 \sum_\sigma \sum_{\substack{\text{over different} \\ \text{links between} \\ \text{the same vertex} \\ \text{pair}}} (e_{\sigma i} e_{\sigma j})^2$$

$$= 2^m \Big\{ \sum \nu_{ij} + 2 \sum \tfrac{1}{2} \nu_{ij} (\nu_{ij} - 1) \Big\}$$

$$= 2^m \sum_M \nu_{ij}{}^2,$$

where the sum is taken over all pairs of variables i,j in M.

We therefore have $\quad H(M) = m \log 2 + \dfrac{\delta^2}{2} \sum_M \nu_{ij}{}^2$,

and similarly $\qquad H(S) = s \log 2 + \dfrac{\delta^2}{2} \sum_S \nu_{ij}{}^2$.

The fact that ν_{ij} appears in this function, squared, means that the distinction between L^+ and L^- will not affect the result. As noted above in Chapter 8 then, we shall proceed without making the distinction between L^+ and L^-, using L alone and assuming that ν_{ij} takes positive values only. It also means, of course, that it is not worth making the distinction between negative and positive interaction, when stating the problem.[11]

Let us now consider an arbitrary partition of M into subsets $S_1, S_2 \cdots S_\mu$, such that $S_\alpha \cap S_\beta = 0$, and $\bigcup_\mu S_\alpha = M$. We shall refer to such a partition, typically, as π.

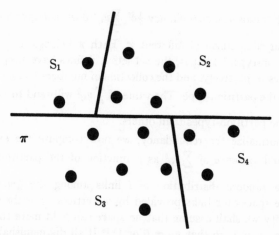

The information contained in M is $H(M)$. The information contained in the S_α taken separately is $\sum_\pi H(S_\alpha)$. Except in the case where there is no interaction at all between the different subsystems, the second of these two expressions will be larger than the first, because some information will, as it were, be counted more than once. As a result, we may use the difference between the two expressions, $\left\{\left[\sum_\pi H(S_\alpha)\right] - H(M)\right\}$ as a measure of the strength of the connections severed by the partition π.[12] The larger it is, the stronger the connections severed are. The smaller it is, the weaker the connections are, and the less information transfer there is across the partition. The value of this difference is given by

$$\left\{ (s_1 + \cdots + s_\mu) \log 2 + \frac{\delta^2}{2} \sum_{S_1, S_2, \ldots} \nu_{ij}{}^2 - m \log 2 - \frac{\delta^2}{2} \sum_M \nu_{ij}{}^2 \right\},$$

where the sum $\displaystyle\sum_{S_1, S_2, \ldots}$ is taken only over pairs i,j, which are wholly contained in one of the S_α. The difference, or redundancy, of the partition is therefore $\frac{1}{2}\delta^2 \sum_\pi \nu_{ij}{}^2$, where the sum is taken over all links ij cut by the partition π.

As it stands the redundancy $\frac{1}{2}\delta^2 \sum_\pi \nu_{ij}^2$ does not give us a fair basis for comparison of different π. Each π belongs to a certain "partition-type." That is, the subsets it defines have $s_1, s_2, \cdots s_\mu$ variables respectively, and the collection of numbers $\{s_1, s_2, \cdots s_\mu\}$ defines the partition-type. The value of $\sum_\pi \nu_{ij}^2$ will tend to be lower for some partition-types than others.

To normalize the redundancy, we now compute the expected value and variance of $\sum_\pi \nu_{ij}^2$ as a function of the partition-type, given a random distribution of l links among the $\frac{1}{2}m(m-1)$ possible spaces for links provided by m vertices. (For the sake of simplicity we shall assume that no space can hold more than one link, i.e., $\nu = 1$, so that $\nu_{ij} = 0$ or 1).[13] If all distinguishable distributions of the l links are equiprobable, the expected value and variance of $\sum_\pi \nu_{ij}^2$ will depend on four parameters. Two of them are constant. The first, l, is the number of links in L. The second, l_0, is the number of possible spaces to which links might be assigned. It is given by $l_0 = \dfrac{m(m-1)}{2}$. The other two parameters depend on the partition π. The first, l_0^π, is the number of the l_0 potential spaces which are cut by the partition π, i.e., the number of vertex pairs in which vertices come from different subsets of the partition. This depends on the partition-type of π, and is given by $l_0^\pi = \sum_\pi s_\alpha s_\beta$, where s_α is the number of variables in S_α. We note that $l_0^\pi \leqslant l_0$. The second of these parameters, l^π, is the number of actual links cut by the partition π. This is given by $l^\pi = \sum_\pi |\nu_{ij}|$. Of course $l^\pi \leqslant l$.

We consider first the expected value of $\sum_\pi \nu_{ij}^2 = \mathrm{E}\left(\sum_\pi \nu_{ij}^2\right)$. Since the ν_{ij} are independent we may write

$$\mathrm{E}\left(\sum_\pi \nu_{ij}^2\right) = \sum_\pi \mathrm{E}(\nu_{ij}^2) = l_0^\pi \mathrm{E}(\nu_{ij}^2),$$

where $\mathrm{E}(\nu_{ij}^2)$ is the expected value of ν_{ij}^2 for some one fixed space spanning two points i,j.

Clearly
$$\mathrm{E}(\nu_{ij}^2) = \frac{l}{l_0},$$

so this reduces to
$$\mathrm{E}\Big(\sum_\pi \nu_{ij}^2\Big) = \frac{ll_0^\pi}{l_0},$$

which depends on the value of l_0^π and so on the partition-type of π.

Let us now consider the variance of $\sum_\pi \nu_{ij}^2$. [14]

$$\mathrm{Var}\,\Big(\sum_\pi \nu_{ij}^2\Big) = \mathrm{E}\Big[\Big(\sum_\pi \nu_{ij}^2\Big)^2\Big] - \Big[\mathrm{E}\Big(\sum_\pi \nu_{ij}^2\Big)\Big]^2.$$

We already know the value of the second term. As for the first:

$$\mathrm{E}\Big[\Big(\sum_\pi \nu_{ij}^2\Big)^2\Big] = \mathrm{E}\Big[\sum_\pi \nu_{ij}^4 + 2\sum_\pi \nu_{ij}^2\nu_{kl}^2\Big].$$

Since we have arranged to take ν_{ij} as positive, $=0$ or 1, we have $\nu_{ij}^4 = \nu_{ij}^2 = \nu_{ij}$ and hence:

$$\mathrm{Var}\,\Big(\sum_\pi \nu_{ij}^2\Big) = \mathrm{E}\Big(\sum_\pi \nu_{ij}\Big) + 2\mathrm{E}\Big(\sum_\pi \nu_{ij}\nu_{kl}\Big) - \Big[\mathrm{E}\Big(\sum_\pi \nu_{ij}\Big)\Big]^2.$$

Let us consider two fixed spaces ij and kl.
Now

$$\begin{aligned}
\mathrm{E}(\nu_{ij}\nu_{kl}) &= 0 \cdot p(\nu_{ij}\nu_{kl} = 0) + 1 \cdot p(\nu_{ij}\nu_{kl} = 1) \\
&= p(\nu_{ij}\nu_{kl} = 1) \\
&= \frac{l}{l_0} \cdot \frac{l-1}{l_0-1} = \frac{l(l-1)}{l_0(l_0-1)}.
\end{aligned}$$

$$\begin{aligned}
\therefore\quad \mathrm{E}\Big(\sum_\pi \nu_{ij}\nu_{kl}\Big) &= \tfrac{1}{2}l_0^\pi(l_0^\pi - 1) \cdot \mathrm{E}(\nu_{ij}\nu_{kl}) \\
&= \tfrac{1}{2}l_0^\pi(l_0^\pi - 1) \cdot \frac{l(l-1)}{l_0(l_0-1)}.
\end{aligned}$$

This gives us

$$\mathrm{Var}\,\Big(\sum_\pi \nu_{ij}^2\Big) = \frac{l \cdot l_0^\pi}{l_0} + l_0(l_0^\pi - 1)\frac{l(l-1)}{l_0(l_0-1)} - \Big(\frac{l \cdot l_0^\pi}{l_0}\Big)^2$$

189

$$= \frac{ll_0{}^\pi}{l_0{}^2 \cdot (l_0 - 1)} \left[l_0{}^2 - l_0 + l_0(l_0{}^\pi - 1)(l - 1) - ll_0{}^\pi(l_0 - 1) \right]$$

$$= \frac{ll_0{}^\pi}{l_0{}^2(l_0 - 1)} \left[l_0{}^2 - l_0 l_0{}^\pi \right] = \frac{ll_0{}^\pi}{l_0(l_0 - 1)} \; (l_0 - l_0{}^\pi).$$

Again the variance depends on the value of $l_0{}^\pi$ and hence on the partition-type of π.

In the case we are considering, where $\nu = 1$, the straightforward redundancy of a partition π, is

$$\tfrac{1}{2}\delta^2 \sum_\pi \nu_{ij}{}^2 = \tfrac{1}{2}\delta^2 l^\pi.$$

To normalize this for different partition-types, we now replace it by [15]

$$R(\pi) = \frac{\text{constant} \cdot [l^\pi - E(l^\pi)]}{[\text{Var } (l^\pi)]^{\frac{1}{2}}} = \frac{\text{constant } [l^\pi - ll_0{}^\pi/l_0]}{[ll_0{}^\pi(l_0 - l_0{}^\pi)/l_0(l_0 - 1)]^{\frac{1}{2}}},$$

and choose the constant to make this

$$\frac{l_0 l^\pi - ll_0{}^\pi}{[l_0{}^\pi(l_0 - l_0{}^\pi)]^{\frac{1}{2}}}.$$

This function has the same expected value and variance for all partition-types, and may therefore be used to compare partitions of all types with one another.

Expressed in terms of the earlier notation, this function is [16]

$$R(\pi) = \frac{\tfrac{1}{2}m(m - 1)\sum_\pi \nu_{ij} - l\sum_\pi s_\alpha s_\beta}{\left[\left(\sum_\pi s_\alpha s_\beta \right)\left(\tfrac{1}{2}m(m - 1) - \sum_\pi s_\alpha s_\beta \right) \right]^{\frac{1}{2}}}.$$

Let us consider, lastly, the practical problem of finding that partition π, of the set M, for which this function $R(\pi)$ takes the smallest (algebraic) value.

To find the best partition of a set S, we use a hill-climbing procedure which consists essentially of taking the partition into one-element subsets, computing the value of $R(\pi)$ for this partition, and then comparing with it all those partitions which can be obtained from it by combining two of its sets. Whichever of these partitions has the lowest value of $R(\pi)$ is then substituted for the original partition; and the procedure continues. It continues until it comes to a partition whose value of $R(\pi)$ is lower than that of any partition which can be obtained from it by combining two sets.

Another hill-climbing procedure, which finds a tree of partitions directly, goes in the opposite direction. It starts with the whole set S, and breaks it into its two most independent disjoint subsets, by computing $R(\pi)$ for a random two-way partition, and improving the partition by moving one variable at a time from side to side, until no further improvement is possible. It then repeats this process for each of the two subsets obtained, breaking each of them into two smaller subsets, and so on iteratively, until the entire set S is decomposed.

These and other methods have been programed for the IBM 7090, and are described in full elsewhere.[17] It is important, and rather surprising, that the techniques do not suffer from the sampling difficulties often found in hill-climbing procedures, but gives extremely stable optima even for short computation times.

Chapter One. The Need for Rationality

1. D. Bullivant, "Information for the Architect," *Architect's Journal*, 129:504–21 (April 1959); Serge Chermayeff and René d'Harnancourt, "Design for Use," in *Art in Progress* (New York, 1944), pp. 190–201.

2. For some practical suggestions as to how this might be improved, see Christopher Alexander, "Information and an Organized Process of Design," in National Academy of Sciences, *Proceedings of the Building Research Institute* (Washington, D.C.), Spring 1961, pp. 115–24.

3. T. W. Cook, "The Relation between Amount of Material and Difficulty of Problem-Solving," *Journal of Experimental Psychology*, 20 (1937):178–83, 288–96; E. J. Archer, L. E. Bourne, Jr., and F. G. Brown, "Concept Identification as a Function of Irrelevant Information and Instructions," *ibid.*, 49 (1955):153–64.

4. This feeling has been expressed in many quarters, ever since the beginning of the Modern Movement. See, for instance, L. Moholy-Nagy, *The New Vision: From Material to Architecture*, revised trans. by Daphne Hoffman (New York, 1947), p. 54; Walter Gropius, *The New Architecture and the Bauhaus*, trans. P. Morton Shand (London, 1935), pp. 17–20.

5. Karl Duncker, "A Qualitative (Experimental and Theoretical) Study of Productive Thinking (Solving of Comprehensible Problems)," *Journal of Genetic Psychology*, 33 (1926): 642–708, and *On Problem Solving*, trans. Lynnes Lees, American Psychological Association, *Psychological Monographs*, No. 270 (Washington, D.C., 1945); Max Wertheimer, *Productive Thinking* (New York, 1945).

6. George A. Miller, "The Magical Number Seven, Plus or Minus Two: Some Limits on Our Capacity for Processing Information," *Psychological Review*, 63 (1956):81–97; D. B. Yntema and G. E. Mueser, "Remembering the Present States of a Number of Variables," *Journal of Experimental Psychology*, 60:18–22 (July 1960).

7. Alex Bavelas and Howard Perlmutter, classified work done at the Center for International Studies, M.I.T., quoted in "The Relation of

Knowledge to Action," by Max Millikan, in *The Human Meaning of the Social Sciences*, ed. Daniel Lerner (New York, 1959), p. 164.

8. In fact there are cases where a form has been uniquely determined by its requirements, but such cases are very rare. One striking example is the crane hook. See L. Bruce Archer, *Design*, No. 90 (June 1956), pp. 12–19, esp. p. 16; H. J. Gough, H. L. Cox, D. G. Sopwith, "The Design of Crane Hooks," *Proceedings of the Institute of Mechanical Engineers* (England), 1935; also Annual Report of the British Iron and Steel Research Association, 1954.

9. A typical collection of paintings based on such a kind of "logical" formalism is to be found in Karl Gerstner, *Kalte Kunst*, published by Arthur Niggli (Teufen AR, Switzerland, 1957).

10. Jacomo Barozzio Vignola, *Regola delli cinque ordini d'architettura* (Rome, 1562; Jacques-François Blondel, *Cours d'architecture* (Paris, 1771), Book IV.

11. Another example of this "logically" inspired formalism is to be found in Ludwig Hilbersheimer, *The New City* (Chicago, 1944), pp. 106–21.

12. Whether we like it or not, however rational we should like to be, there is a factor of judgment in the choice and use of a logical system which we cannot avoid. Logical pictures, like any others, are made by simplification and selection. It is up to us to see which simplifications we wish to make, which aspects to select as significant, which picture to adopt. And this decision is logically arbitrary. However reasonable and sound the picture is internally, the choice of a picture must be, in the end, irrational. For even if we can give reasons for choosing one logical scheme rather than another, these reasons only imply that there is another decision scheme behind the first (very likely not explicit). Perhaps there is still another behind this second one. But somewhere there are decisions made that are not rational in any sense, that are subject to nothing more than the personal bias of the decision maker. *Logical methods, at best, rearrange the way in which personal bias is to be introduced into a problem.* Of course, this "at best" is rather important. Present intuitive methods unhappily introduce personal bias in such a way that it makes problems impossible to solve correctly. Our purpose must be to repattern the bias, so that it no longer interferes in this destructive way with the process of design, and no longer inhibits clarity of form.

13. The relevant part of William Morris' thinking is to be found in volumes 22 and 23 of the 1915 London edition of his complete works. See also Nikolaus Pevsner, *Pioneers of Modern Design* (New York, 1949), pp. 24–30.

14. *Ibid.*, pp. 18–19.

15. Their work and ideas are fully discussed by Emil Kaufmann in

Architecture and the Age of Reason (Cambridge, Mass., 1955), pp. 95–99 and 134. No writings of Lodoli's remain, but see F. Algarotti, *Saggio sopra l'architettura*, in *Opere*, vol. II (Livorno, 1764); Marc-Antoine Laugier, *Essai sur l'architecture*, 2nd ed. (Paris, 1775), and *Observations sur l'architecture* (The Hague, 1765).

16. Nicolaus Pevsner, *An Outline of European Architecture*, Penguin Books (London, 1953), pp. 242–62.

17. In denying the possibility of understanding reasonably the processes of form production, the fetish of intuition is closely parallel to other famous attempts to shelter from the loss of innocence under the wings of magic and taboo; see, for comments, Sigmund Freud, *Civilization and Its Discontents*, trans. James Strachey (New York, 1962), or K. R. Popper in *The Open Society and Its Enemies* (Princeton, 1950).

18. For some recent protests against the willful nature of modern intuition in design, see Serge Chermayeff, "The Shape of Quality," *Architecture Plus* (Division of Architecture, A. & M. College of Texas), 2 (1959–60):16–23.

19. The possibility of amplifying intelligence has already been hinted at in W. Ross Ashby, "Design for an Intelligence Amplifier," in *Automata Studies*, ed. C. E. Shannon and J. McCarthy (Princeton, 1956), pp. 215–34. See also M. Minsky, "Steps towards Artificial Intelligence," *Proceedings of the Institute of Radio Engineers*, 49:8–30 (January 1961).

Chapter Two. Goodness of Fit

1. The source of form actually lies in the fact that the world tries to compensate for its irregularities as economically as possible. This principle, sometimes called the principle of least action, has been noted in various fields: notably by Le Chatelier, who observed that chemical systems tend to react to external forces in such a way as to neutralize the forces; also in mechanics as Newton's law, as Lenz's law in electricity, again as Volterra's theory of populations. See Adolph Mayer, *Geschichte des Prinzips der kleinsten Action* (Leipzig, 1877).

2. D'Arcy Wentworth Thompson, *On Growth and Form*, 2nd ed. (Cambridge, 1959), p. 16.

3. This old idea is at least as old as Plato: see, e.g., *Gorgias* 474–75.

4. The symmetry of this situation (i.e., the fact that adaptation is a mutual phenomenon referring to the context's adaptation to the form as much as to the form's adaptation to its context) is very important. See L. J. Henderson, *The Fitness of the Environment* (New York, 1913), page v: "Darwinian fitness is compounded of a mutual relationship between the organism and the environment." Also E. H. Starling's remark, "Organism and environment form a whole, and must be viewed

as such." For a beautifully concise description of the concept "form," see Albert M. Dalcq, "Form and Modern Embryology," in *Aspects of Form*, ed. Lancelot Whyte (London, 1951), pp. 91–116, and other articles in the same symposium.

5. At later points in the text where I use the word "system," this always refers to the whole ensemble. However, some care is required here, since many writers refer to that part of the ensemble which is held constant as the environment, and call only the part under adjustment the "system." For these writers my form, not my ensemble, would be the system.

6. In essence this is a very old idea. It was the first clearly formulated by Darwin in *The Origin of Species*, and has since been highly developed by such writers as W. B. Cannon, *The Wisdom of the Body* (London, 1932), and W. Ross Ashby, *Design for a Brain*, 2nd ed. (New York, 1960).

7. Wolfgang Köhler, *The Place of Value in a World of Facts* (New York, 1938), p. 96.

8. A. D. de Groot, "Über das Denken des Schachspielers," *Rivista di psicologia*, 50:90–91 (October–December 1956). Ludwig Wittgenstein, *Philosophical Investigations* (Oxford, 1953), p. 15.

9. See Max Wertheimer, "Zu dem Problem der Unterscheidung von Einzelinhalt und Teil," *Zeitschrift für Psychologie*, 129 (1933):356, and "On Truth," *Social Research*, 1:144 (May 1934).

10. K. Lönberg Holm and C. Theodore Larsen, *Development Index* (Ann Arbor, 1953), p. Ib.

11. Again, this idea is not a new one. It was certainly present in Frank Lloyd Wright's use of the phrase "organic architecture," for example, though on his tongue the phrase contained so many other intentions that it is hard to understand it clearly. For a good discussion see Peter Collins, "Biological Analogy," *Architectural Review*, 126:303–6 (December 1959).

12. This observation appears with beautiful clarity in Ozenfant's *Foundations of Modern Art* (New York, 1952), pp. 340–41. Also Kurt Koffka, *Principles of Gestalt Psychology* (London, 1935), pp. 638–44.

13. The idea that the residual patterns of adaptive processes are intrinsically well organized is expressed by W. Ross Ashby in *Design for a Brain*, p. 233, and by Norbert Wiener in *The Human Use of Human Beings* (New York, 1954), p. 37.

14. See note 2.

15. The concept of an image, comparable to the ideal field statement of a problem, is discussed at great length in G. A. Miller, Eugene Galanter, and Karl H. Pribram, *Plans and the Structure of Behavior* (New York, 1960). The "image" is presented there as something present in

every problem solver's mind, and used by him as a criterion for the problem's solution and hence as the chief guide in problem planning and solving. It seems worth making a brief comment. In the majority of interesting cases I do not believe that such an image exists psychologically, so that the testing paradigm described by Miller et al. in *Plans* is therefore an incorrect description of complex problem-solving behavior. In interesting cases the solution of the problem cannot be tested against an image, because the search for the image or criterion for success is actually going on at the same time as the search for a solution.

Miller does make a brief comment acknowledging this possibility on pp. 171–72. He also agreed to this point in personal discussions at Harvard in 1961.

16. It is not hard to see why, if this is so, the concept of good fit is relatively hard to grasp. It has been shown by a number of investigators, for example, Jerome Bruner et al., *A Study of Thinking* (New York, 1958), that people are very unwilling and slow to accept disjunctive concepts. To be told what something is not is of very little use if you are trying to find out what it is. See pp. 156–81. See also C. L. Hovland and W. Weiss, "Transmission of Information Concerning Concepts through Positive and Negative Instances," *Journal of Experimental Psychology*, 45 (1953):175–82.

17. The near identity of "force" on the one hand, and the "requiredness" generated by the context on the other, is discussed fully in Köhler, *The Place of Value in a World of Facts*, p. 345, and throughout pp. 329–60. There is, to my mind, a striking similarity between the difficulty of dealing with good fit directly, in spite of its primary importance, and the difficulty of the concept zero. Zero and the concept of emptiness, too, are comparatively late inventions (clearly because they too leave one nothing to hold onto in explaining them). Even now we find it hard to conceive of emptiness as such: we only manage to think of it as the absence of something positive. Yet in many metaphysical systems, notably those of the East, emptiness and absence are regarded as more fundamental and ultimately more substantial than presence.

This is also connected with the fact, now acknowledged by most biologists, that symmetry, being the natural condition of an unstressed situation, does not require explanation, but that on the contrary it is asymmetry which needs to be explained. See D'Arcy Thompson, *On Growth and Form*, p. 357; Wilhelm Ludwig, *Recht-links-problem im Tierreich und beim Menschen* (Berlin, 1932); Hermann Weyl, *Symmetry* (Princeton, 1952), pp. 25–26; Ernst Mach, "Über die physikalische Bedeutung der Gesetze der Symmetrie," *Lotos*, 21 (1871):139–47.

18. The logical equivalence of these two views is expressed by De

Morgan's law, which says essentially that if A, B, C, etc., are propositions, then [(Not A) and (Not B) and (Not C) . . .] is always the same as Not [(A or B or C or . . .)].

19. For the idea that departures from closure force themselves on the attention more strikingly than closure itself, and are actually the primary data of a certain kind of evaluative experience, and for a number of specific examples (not only ethical), see Max Wertheimer, "Some Problems in Ethics," *Social Research*, 2: 352ff (August 1935). In particular, what I have been describing as misfits are described there as *Leerstellen* or emptinesses. The feeling that something is missing, and the need to fill whatever is incomplete (*Lückenfüllung*), are discussed in some detail.

20. Any psychological theory which treats perception or cognition as information processing is bound to come to the same kind of conclusion. For a typical discussion of such information-reducing processes, see Bruner et al., *A Study of Thinking*, p. 166.

21. It is perhaps instructive to note that both the concept of organic health in medicine and the concept of psychological normality in psychiatry are subject to the same kind of difficulties as my conception of a well-fitting form or coherent ensemble. In their respective professions they are considered to be well defined. Yet the only definitions that can be given are of a negative kind. See, for instance, Sir Geoffrey Vickers, "The Concept of Stress in Relation to the Disorganization of Human Behavior," in *Stress and Psychiatric Disorder*, ed. J. M. Tanner (Oxford, 1960).

22. In case it seems doubtful whether all the relevant properties of an ensemble can be expressed as variables, let us be quite clear about the fact that these variables are not necessarily capable of continuous variation. Indeed, it is quite obvious that most of the issues which occur in a design problem cannot be treated numerically, as this would require. A binary variable is simply a formal shorthand way of classifying situations; it is an indicator which distinguishes between forms that work and those that do not, in a given context.

Chapter Three: The Source of Good Fit

1. Alan Houghton Brodrick, "Grass Roots," *Architectural Review*, 115:101–11 (February 1954); W. G. Sumner, *Folkways* (Boston, 1908), p. 2. The same point is made by Adolf Loos in his famous story of the saddle-maker, *Trotzdem*, 2nd ed. (Innsbruck, 1931), pp. 13–14; to be found translated by Eduard Sekler in *Journal of Architectural Education*, vol. 12, no. 2 (Summer 1957), p. 31.

2. Ludwig Hilbersheimer, *Mies van der Rohe* (Chicago, 1956), p. 63.

3. Robert W. Marks, *The Dymaxion World of Buckminster Fuller* (New York, 1960), pp. 110–33.

4. Peter Collins, "Not with Steel and Cement," *Manchester Guardian Weekly*, January 14, 1960.

5. Office de la Recherche Scientifique Outre-Mer, *L'Habitat aux Cameroun* (Paris, 1952), p. 35.

6. *Ibid.*, p. 38.

7. *Ibid.*, p. 34.

8. See this chapter, p. 28.

9. Brodrick, " Grass Roots," p. 101.

10. In case this needs justification as a procedure, it is worth pointing out perhaps that the concept of "economic man," which underlay more than a century of economic theory, was admitted to be no more than a useful explanatory fiction. More recently, Robert Redfield has made much the same suggestion in "The Folk Society," *American Journal of Sociology*, 52:293–308 (January 1947), where he puts forward the "ideal" primitive society as a mental construct which serves a useful basis for comparison.

11. A. R. Radcliffe-Brown, "The Mother's Brother in South Africa," *South African Journal of Science*, 21 (1925):544–45.

12. Redfield, "The Folk Society," p. 293.

13. K. R. Popper, *The Open Society and Its Enemies* (Princeton, 1950), p. 169.

14. Sybil Moholy-Nagy, *Native Genius in Anonymous Architecture* (New York, 1957), throughout.

15. Of course, although selfconsciousness, as I shall define it, does tend to affect many aspects of culture at once, we certainly know of cases where cultures are highly selfconscious in some respects, yet quite unselfconscious in others. It is especially important to avoid any suggestion of evolution here (to the effect that all cultures are at first unselfconscious, and become uniformly less so as they grow more mature). The fact is that selfconsciousness is differently directed in different cultures; some peoples give their closest attention to one sort of thing, some to another. This is excellently demonstrated by Marcel Mauss in "Les Techniques du corps," *Journal de psychologie*, 32 (1935):271–93.

16. Sumner, *Folkways*, pp. 3–4; Lucien Lévy-Bruhl, *How Natives Think* (New York, 1925), pp. 109–16, 127; Roger Brown, *Words and Things* (Glencoe, Ill., 1958), pp. 272–73; B. L. Whorf, "Linguistic Factors in the Terminology of Hopi Architecture," *International Journal of American Linguistics*, 19 (1953):141.

17. Redfield, "The Folk Society," pp. 297, 299–300, 303. For further specific examples, see, for instance, Margaret Mead, "Art and Reality,"

College Art Journal, 2:119 (May 1943); A. I. Richards, *Land, Labour and Diet in Northern Rhodesia* (Oxford, 1939), pp. 230–34, and "Huts and Hut-Building among the Bemba," *Man*, 50 (1950):89; Raymond Firth, *We the Tikopia* (London, 1936), pp. 75–80; Clyde Kluckhohn and Dorothea Leighton, *The Navaho* (Cambridge, Mass., 1946), p. 46.

18. For a rather extreme description of this kind of education, see B. F. Skinner, *The Behavior of Organisms* (New York, 1938). A more balanced discussion of the growth of feeling for a skill is to be found in J. L. Gillin and J. P. Gillin, *Cultural Sociology* (New York, 1948), p. 80.

19. *Ibid.*, pp. 400–3.

20. *Ibid.*, pp. 403–4.

21. Jerome Bruner, *The Process of Education* (Cambridge, Mass., 1960), p. 24.

22. The distinction between implicit rules and explicit rules is explored at some length by E. T. Hall in *The Silent Language* (New York, 1959), pp. 69–74 and 91–95.

23. It has been common, ever since the great Paris exhibition of primitive art at the turn of the century, to claim all sorts of things for the primitive artists—that they are more sensitive than we, more highly developed as artists, etc. The same thought appears in Barbara Hutton, *The Unsophisticated Arts* (London, 1945). I am profoundly skeptical. The secret of the primitive form-builders' success lies not in the men themselves, but in the process of design they are accustomed to. Willy-nilly they are caught up in a process of design which produces good form *on account of the organization of the process*. Similar skepticism is to be found in Ralph Linton, "Primitive Art," *The Kenyon Review*, 3:34–51 (Winter 1941).

24. See, typically, Sumner, *Folkways*, p. 54; A. R. Radcliffe-Brown, *Structure and Function in Primitive Society* (Glencoe, Ill., 1952), pp. 7–9.

25. The archeological evidence is so thin that any pseudo-Darwinian accounts based on it cannot be more than highly general and rather doubtful fictions. Radcliffe-Brown, *Structure and Function in Primitive Society*, pp. 202–3.

26. To see that this kind of assumption, implicit throughout the writings of Lewis Morgan, for example, is unjustified, see Radcliffe-Brown, *Structure and Function in Primitive Society*, p. 203.

27. The concept of homeostasis was first used extensively by W. B. Cannon in *The Wisdom of the Body* (London, 1932). For a precise definition see W. Ross Ashby, *Design for a Brain*, 2nd ed. (New York, 1960), chapter 5. And for a number of discussions see *Self-Organizing Systems*, ed. Marshall Yovits and Scott Cameron (New York, 1960). For a de-

tailed descriptive discussion see also H. von Foerster, "Basic Concepts of Homeostasis," *Homeostatic Mechanisms*, Brookhaven Symposia in Biology, No. 10 (Upton, N.Y., 1957), pp. 216–42.

28. This example is based on one given in Ashby, *Design for a Brain*, p. 151.

29. *Ibid.*

30. See Chapter 9, note 4.

31. Ashby, pp. 192–204.

32. As Ashby puts it, "For the accumulation of adaptations to be possible, the system must not be fully joined" (p. 155).

33. This behavior of the misfits may be represented in step-function form. See Ashby, pp. 87–90.

34. This would correspond to what Ashby calls ultrastability, *ibid.*, pp. 122–37.

Chapter Four: The Unselfconscious Process

1. By the definition of Chapter 3, p. 36.

2. Alexander Scharff, *Archeologische Beiträge zur Frage der Entstehung der Hieroglyphenschrift* (Munich, 1942), and "Ägypten," in *Handbuch der Archäologie*, ed. Walter Otto (Munich, 1937), pp. 431–642, especially pp. 437–38.

3. L. G. Bark, "Beehive Dwellings of Apulia," *Antiquity*, 6 (1932): 410.

4. Werner Kissling, "House Traditions in the Outer Hebrides," *Man*, 44 (1944): 137; H. A. and B. H. Huscher, "The Hogan Builders of Colorado," *Southwestern Lore*, 9 (1943): 1–92.

5. In the *Song of Songs* i. 5 we find, "I am black, but comely, O ye daughters of Jerusalem, as the tents of Kedar . . .," and *Exodus* contains many colorful descriptions of the tabernacle (the legendary form of the tent): xxvi.14, "And thou shalt make a covering for the tent of rams' skins dyed red, and a covering above of badgers' skins," and xxvi.36, "And thou shalt make an hanging for the door of the tent, of blue, and purple, and scarlet, and fine twined linen, wrought with needlework." C. G. Peilberg, "La Tente noire," *Nationalmuseets Skrifter*, Etnografisk Raekke, Vol. 2 (Copenhagen, 1944), pp. 205–9.

6. All houses in county Kerry have two doors, but you must always leave by the door you entered by, since a man who comes in through one and goes out through the other takes the house's luck away with him. Åke Campbell, "Notes on the Irish House," *Folk-Liv* (Stockholm), 2 (1938): 192; E. E. Evans, "Donegal Survivals," *Antiquity*, 13 (1939): 212.

7. Thomas Whiffen, *The North-West Amazons* (London, 1915), p. 225.

And the same is true of many other peoples. For instance: Gunnar Landtman, "The Folk Tales of the Kiwai Papuans," *Acta Societatis Scientiarum Fennicae* (Helsinki), 47 (1917):116, and "Papuan Magic in the Building of Houses," *Acta Academiae Aboensis, Humaniora,* 1 (1920):5.

8. Margaret Mead, *An Inquiry into the Question of Cultural Stability in Polynesia*, Columbia University Contributions to Anthropology, Vol. 9 (New York, 1928), pp. 45, 50, 57, 68–69.

9. The blessing way rite, a collection of legends and prayers, makes a positive link between their world view and the shape of the dwelling by relating the parts of the hogan, fourfold, to the four points of the compass, and by referring to them, always, in the order of the sun's path—east, south, west, north. Thus one song describes the hogan's structure: "A white bead pole in the east, a turquoise pole in the south, an abalone pole in the west, a jet pole in the north." The ritual involved in the hogan's use goes further still, so far that it even gives details of how ashes should be taken from the hogan fire. Berard Haile, "Some Cultural Aspects of the Navaho Hogan," mimeographed, Dept. of Anthropology, University of Chicago, 1937, pp. 5–6, and "Why the Navaho Hogan," *Primitive Man*, Vol. 15, Nos. 3–4 (1942), pp. 41–42.

10. Hiroa Te Rangi (P. H. Buck), *Samoan Material Culture*, Bernice P. Bishop Museum Bulletin No. 75 (Honolulu, 1930), p. 19.

11. L. G. Bark, "Beehive Dwellings of Apulia," p. 409.

12. William Edwards, "To Build a Hut," *The South Rhodesia Native Affairs Department Annual* (Salisbury, Rhodesia), No. 6 (1928):73–74.

13. Iowerth C. Peate, *The Welsh House*, Honorary Society of Cymmrodorion (London, 1940), pp. 183–90.

14. H. Frobenius, *Oceanische Bautypen* (Berlin, 1899), p. 12.

15. Campbell, "Notes on the Irish House," p. 223.

16. Clark Wissler, "Material Culture of the Blackfoot Indians," *Anthropological Papers of the American Museum of History*, Vol. 5, part 1 (New York, 1910), p. 99.

17. L. G. Bark, "Beehive Dwellings of Apulia," p. 408.

18. A. I. Richards, "Huts and Hut-Building among the Bemba," *Man*, 50 (1950):89.

19. It is true that craftsmen do appear in certain cultures which we should want to call unselfconscious (e.g., carpenters in the Marquesas, thatchers in South Wales), but their effect is never more than partial. They have no monopoly on skill, but simply do what they do rather better than most other men. And while thatchers or carpenters may be employed during the *construction* of the house, repairs are still undertaken by the owner. The skills needed are universal, and at some level or other practiced by everyone. Ralph Linton, *Material Culture of the Marquesas,*

Bernice P. Bishop Museum Memoirs, Vol. 8., No. 5 (Honolulu, 1923), p. 268. Peate, *The Welsh House*, pp. 201–5.

20. Barr Ferree, "Climatic Influence in Primitive Architecture," *The American Anthropologist*, 3 (1890):149.

21. Richard King, "On the Industrial Arts of the Esquimaux," *Journal of the Ethnological Society of London*, 1 (1848):281–82. Diamond Jenness, *Report of the Canadian Arctic Expedition (1913–1918)*, vol. 12: *The Life of the Copper Eskimos* (Ottawa, 1922), p. 63; J. Gabus, "La Construction des iglous chez les Padleirmiut," *Bulletin de la Société Neuchateloise de Géographie*, 47 (1939–40):43–51. D. B. Marsh, "Life in a Snowhouse," *Natural History*, 60.2:66 (February 1951).

22. W. G. Sumner, *Folkways*, p. 2.

23. Jenness, *Copper Eskimos*, p. 60.

24. W. McClintock, "The Blackfoot Tipi," *Southwestern Museum Leaflets*, No. 5 (Los Angeles, 1936), pp. 6–7.

25. Not only are the walls themselves daubed whenever they need to be, but whole rooms are added and subtracted whenever the accommodation is felt to be inadequate or superfluous. Meyer Fortes, *The Web of Kinship among the Tallensi* (London, 1949), pp. 47–50. Jack Goody, "The Fission of Domestic Groups among the LoDagoba," in *The Development Cycle in Domestic Groups*, ed. J. Goody (Cambridge, 1958), p. 80.

26. Whiffen, *The North-West Amazons*, p. 41.

27. Norbert Wiener, *Cybernetics* (New York, 1948), pp. 113–36.

28. *Ibid.*, pp. 121–22; Ross Ashby, *Design for a Brain* (New York, 1960), pp. 100–4.

29. Strictly speaking, what we have shown concerns only the *reaction* of the unselfconscious culture to misfit. We have not yet explained the occurrence of good fit in the first place. But all we need to explain it, now, is the inductive argument. We must assume that there was once a very simple situation in which forms fitted well. Once this had occurred, the tradition and directness of the unselfconscious system would have maintained the fit over all later changes in culture.

Since the moment of accidental fit may have been in the remotest prehistoric past, when the culture was in its infancy (and good fit an easy matter on account of the culture's simplicity), the assumption is not a taxing one.

30. This is an obvious point. In another context Pericles put it nicely: "Although only a few may originate a policy, we are all able to judge it." Thucydides ii.41.

31. I am indebted to E. H. Gombrich for drawing my attention to this phenomenon. The interpretation is mine.

Chapter Five: The Selfconscious Process

1. Thus selfconsciousness can arise as a natural outcome of scientific and technological development, by imposition from a conquering culture, by infiltration as in the underdeveloped countries today. See Bruno Snell, *The Discovery of the Mind*, trans. T. G. Rosenmeyer (Cambridge, Mass., 1953), chapter 10, "The Origin of Scientific Thought."

2. Hiroa Te Rangi (P. H. Buck), *Samoan Material Culture*, Bernice P. Bishop Museum Bulletin No. 75 (Honolulu, 1930), pp. 85–86.

3. *Ibid.*, p. 86.

4. For discussion of this development in present-day architecture see Serge Chermayeff, "The Shape of Quality," *Architecture Plus* (Division of Architecture, A. & M. College of Texas), 2 (1959–60):16–23. For an astute and comparatively early comment of this kind, see J. M. Richards, "The Condition of Architecture, and the Principle of Anonymity," in *Circle*, ed. J. L. Martin, Ben Nicholson, and Naum Gabo (London, 1937), pp. 184–89.

5. In Chapter 3, an architecturally selfconscious culture was defined as one in which the rules and precepts of design have been made explicit. In Western Europe technical training of a formal kind began roundabout the mid-fifth century B.C. And the architectural academies themselves were introduced in the late Renaissance. Werner Jaeger, *Paideia*, Vol. I (New York, 1945), pp. 314–16; H. M. Colvin, *A Biographical Dictionary of English Architects, 1660–1840* (Cambridge, Mass., 1954), p. 16. It is of course no accident that the first of these two periods coincided with the prime of Plato's academy (the first establishment where intellectual self-criticism was welcomed and invited), and also with the first extensive recognition of the architect as an individual with a name, and the second with the first widespread crop of architectural treatises. F. M. Cornford, *Before and After Socrates* (Cambridge, 1932); Eduard Sekler, "Der Architekt im Wandel der Zeiten," *Der Aufbau*, 14:486, 489 (December 1959).

6. For a detailed account of the origin and growth of the academies, see the monograph by Nicolaus Pevsner, *Academies of Art* (Cambridge, 1940), esp. pp. 1–24, 243–95.

7. Margaret Mead, "Art and Reality," *College Art Journal*, 2:119 (May 1943); Ralph Linton, "Primitive Art," *Kenyon Review*, 3:42 (Winter 1941).

8. Ralph Linton, *The Study of Man* (New York, 1936), p. 311.

9. See Chapter 3, pp. 41–42.

10. The invention and use of concepts seems to be common to most human problem-solving behavior. Jerome Bruner et al., *A Study of Thinking* (New York, 1956), pp. 10–17. For a description of this process

as re-encoding, see George A. Miller, "The Magical Number Seven, Plus or Minus Two: Some Limits on our Capacity for Processing Information," *Psychological Review*, 63 (1956):108.

11. See, for instance, American Association of State Highway Officials, *A Policy on Geometric Design of Rural Highways* (Washington, D.C., 1954), Contents; or F. R. S. Yorke, *Specification* (London, 1959), p. 3; or E. E. Seelye, *Specification and Costs*, vol. II (New York, 1957), pp. xv–xviii.

12. John Summerson, "The Case for a Theory of Modern Architecture," *Royal Institute of British Architects Journal* 64:307–11 (June 1957).

13. Serge Chermayeff and Christopher Alexander, *Community and Privacy* (New York, 1963), pp. 159–175.

14. Reginald R. Isaacs, "The Neighborhood Theory: An Analysis of Its Adequacy," *Journal of the American Institute of Planners*, 14.2:15–23 (Spring 1948).

15. For a complete treatment of this subject, see Rudolph Carnap, *Meaning and Necessity* (Chicago, 1956). See esp. pp. 23–42, and for a summary see pp. 202–4.

16. *Ibid.*, p. 45.

17. It could be argued possibly that the word "acoustics" is not arbitrary but corresponds to a clearly objective collection of requirements — namely those which deal with auditory phenomena. But this only serves to emphasize its arbitrariness. After all, what has the fact that we happen to have ears got to do with the problem's causal structure?

18. For the fullest treatment of the arbitrariness of language, as far as its descriptions of the world are concerned, and the dependence of such descriptions on the internal structure of the language, see B. L. Whorf, "The Relation of Habitual Thought and Behavior to Language," in *Language, Culture and Personality: Essays in Memory of Edward Sapir*, ed. Leslie Spier (Menasha, Wis., 1941), pp. 75–93.

19. L. Carmichael, H. P. Hogan, and A. A. Walter, "An Experimental Study of the Effect of Language on the Reproduction of Visually Perceived Form," *Journal of Experimental Psychology*, 15 (1932):73–86.

20. Whorf, "Relation of Habitual Thought and Behavior to Language," p. 76. Whorf, who worked for a time as a fire insurance agent, found that certain fires were started because workmen, though careful with matches and cigarettes when they were near full gasoline drums, became careless near empty ones. Actually the empty drums, containing vapor, are more dangerous then the relatively inert full drums. But the word "empty" carries with it the idea of safety, while the word "full" seems to suggest pregnant danger. Thus the concepts "full" and "empty" actually reverse the real structure of the situation, and hence lead to fire.

The effect of concepts on the structure of architectural problems is much the same. *Ibid.*, pp. 75–76. See also Ludwig Wittgenstein, *The Blue and Brown Books* (Oxford, 1958), pp. 17–20.

21. Vitruvius, *De architectura* 3.1, 3, 4. E. R. De Zurko, *Origins of Functionalist Theory* (New York, 1957), pp. 26–28.

22. Werner Sombart, quoted in *Intellectual and Cultural History of the Western World*, by Harry Elmer Barnes (New York, 1937), p. 509: "Ideas of profit seeking and economic rationalism first became possible with the invention of double entry book-keeping. Through this system can be grasped but one thing — the increase in the amount of values considered purely quantitatively. Whoever becomes immersed in double entry book-keeping must forget all qualities of goods and services, abandon the limitations of the need-covering principle, and be filled with the single idea of profit; he may not think of boots and cargoes, of meal and cotton, but only of amounts of values, increasing or diminishing." What is more, these concepts even shut out requirements very close to the center of the intended meaning! Thus in the case of "economics" even such obvious misfit variables as the cost of maintenance and depreciation have only recently been made the subject of architectural consideration. See J. C. Weston, "Economics of Building," *Royal Institute of British Architects Journal*, 62:256–57 (April 1955), 63:268–78 (May 1956), 63:316–29 (June 1956). As for the cost of social overheads — the milkman's rounds; the laundries and TB sanatoria which have to cope with the effects of smoke from open fireplaces — even the economists are only just beginning to consider these. See Benjamin Higgins, *Economic Development* (New York, 1959), pp. 254–56, 660–61. Yet the cost of the form is found in all these things. The true cost of a form is much more complicated than the concept "economics" at first suggests.

Chapter Six: The Program

1. John von Neumann and Oscar Morgenstern, *Theory of Games and Economic Behavior* (Princeton, 1944); Allen Newell, J. C. Shaw, and H. A. Simon, "Chess-Playing Programs and the Problem of Complexity," *IBM Journal of Research and Development*, 2:320–35 (October 1958); Hao Wang, "Toward Mechanical Mathematics," *IBM Journal of Research and Development*, 4:2–22 (January 1960); A. S. Luchins, *Mechanization in Problem Solving*, American Psychological Association, *Psychological Monographs*, No. 248 (Washington, D.C., 1942); Allen Newell, J. C. Shaw, and H. A. Simon, "Elements of a Theory of Human Problem Solving," *Psychological Review*, 65 (1958):151–66.

2. Marvin Minsky, "Heuristic Aspects of the Artificial Intelligence

Problem," Group Reports 34–55, Lincoln Laboratory, M.I.T., 1956, and "Steps towards Artificial Intelligence," *Proceedings of the Institute of Radio Engineers*, 49:8–30 (January 1961). For further references, see Donald T. Campbell, "Blind Variation and Selective Retention in Creative Thought as in Other Knowledge Processes," *Psychological Review*, vol. 67 (1960), esp. pp. 392–95.

3. See Chapter 7, p. 90. Also Chapter 2, p. 20.

4. See, for instance, Karl R. Popper, *The Logic of Scientific Discovery* (New York, 1959), pp. 53–54, 136–45, 278–81; George Polya, *Patterns of Plausible Inference* (Princeton, 1953); Nelson Goodman, *Fact, Fiction, and Forecast* (Cambridge, Mass., 1955), pp. 82-120; W. Pitts and W. S. McCulloch, "How We Know Universals," *Bulletin of Mathematical Biophysics*, 9 (1947):124–47.

5. There are many speculations about the nature of this process in the literature. See such books as Brewster Ghiselin, *The Creative Process* (Berkeley, 1952), and Paul Souriau, *Théorie de l'invention* (Paris, 1881).

6. From the failure of selfconsciousness we might argue first that we should dispense with the designer altogether, and should therefore make the self-organizing character of the unselfconscious ensemble our point of departure. With this end in mind, we might concentrate on giving the ensemble inself properites which would enhance its power to effect internal adaptations. In a trivial sense we already do this when we fit a steam engine with a governor. The regulation of a series of dams or a production line by means of automatic electronic control is a more elaborate example of the same thing. Providing a city with a governmental structure which lets the administration get things done fast is another example. In the future it may even be possible to give cities a physical organization that encourages them to grow and to adapt to new conditions better than they do at present. Cf. Lancelot Whyte, "Some Thoughts on the Design of Nature and Their Implication for Education," *Arts and Architecture*, 73:16–17 (January 1956). All these devices take the burden off selfconscious control and design, because, like the unselfconscious process, they tend to make the ensemble self-organizing.

The drawback of such devices is that they are only useful in very special and limited situations. Their application demands even greater grasp of the ensemble's condition than the selfconscious designer requires. When we come across unfamiliar circumstances where they cannot be applied, there is no alternative to inventiveness; and we must acknowledge something which has so far perhaps not been brought out strongly enough: the human brain is, in spite of its drawbacks, potentially capable of much deeper insight and resolution than anything an external self-organizing process can achieve. Its great potential strength lies in the fact that it derives forms from a conceptual picture of the ensemble, rather than from the ensemble itself. This allows a much wider range of more flexible and intricate forms to develop than does the unselfconscious process, whose forms must always be of a type which can emerge from the everyday events of the real-world ensemble.

7. For a quick introduction to set theory, see Paul R. Halmos, *Naive Set Theory* (New York, 1960). More complete discussion of the theory is to be found in Felix Hausdorff, *Set Theory*, trans. J. R. Aumann (New York, 1957).

8. See the axiom of specification, Halmos, *Naive Set Theory*, p. 6. For the ideas which follow, see *ibid.*, pp. 2, 3, 12, 14.

9. It is commonly understood among designers that the first task in dealing with a design problem is to strip the definition of the problem down to practical terms, to decide just what conditions a successful form must meet. As one designer, Louis Kahn, puts it, when he wants to know what the form really has to do, he asks himself, "what the form wants to be." The set *M* is just a precise way of summarizing the elements of what the form wants to be.

10. See pp. 38–45, 64–66.

11. The main works on graph theory are Denes König, *Theorie der endlichen and unendlichen Graphen* (New York, 1950), Claude Berge, *Théorie des graphes et ses applications* (Paris, 1958), which has now been translated (London, 1962), and Oystein Ore, *Theory of Graphs*, American Mathematical Society Colloquium Publications, vol. 38 (Providence, 1962). See also, as a brief introduction, Frank Harary and Robert Z. Norman, *Graph Theory as a Mathematical Model in Social Science* (Ann Arbor, 1955).

12. In a sense the web of this graph might be regarded as an explicit version of what designers and artists have often talked about as the "internal logic" of a problem.

13. A decomposition is a special case of a partly ordered system; for which see Garrett Birkhoff, *Lattice Theory*, American Mathematical Society Colloquium Publications, vol. 25 (New York, 1948), pp. 1–2.

14. For a discussion of the part played by conceptual hierarchies in cognitive behavior, see George A. Miller, Eugene Galanter, and Karl H. Pribram, *Plans and the Structure of Behavior* (New York, 1960), p. 16.

15. The word "program" has occurred a great deal in the recent literature on the psychology of problem solving — the implication throughout being that man's natural way of solving complex problems is to make them easier for himself by means of heuristics which lead him to a solution stepwise. A. D. de Groot, "Über das Denken des Schachspielers," *Revista di psicologia*, 50:89–90 (October-December 1956); Newell, Shaw, and Simon, "Elements of a Theory of Human Problem Solving," pp. 151–66; Miller et al., *Plans and the Structure of Behavior*, throughout;

James G. March and Herbert A. Simon, *Organizations* (New York, 1958), pp. 190–91. It is interesting that John Summerson recently singled out the fact of programs' being used as a source of architectural unity as the distinguishing feature of modern architecture. "The Case for a Theory of Modern Architecture," *Royal Institute of British Architects Journal,* 64:307–11 (June 1957).

Chapter Seven: The Realization of the Program

1. I owe the word "realization" to Louis Kahn, who has used it extensively, and often with a rather wider meaning; his whole teaching revolves about the point discussed in this chapter. See Louis Kahn, "Concluding Talk," in Oscar Newman, ed., *New Frontiers in Architecture: CIAM '59 in Otterlo* (New York, 1961), pp. 205–16.

2. For this photograph, taken by Professor H. Edgerton, Massachusetts Institute of Technology, see, for instance, Gyorgy Kepes, *The New Landscape* (Chicago, 1956), p. 288.

3. See Le Corbusier and Pierre Jeanneret, *Oeuvres complètes, 1934–1938* (Zurich, 1939), pp. 142–47, and Le Corbusier, *La Ville radieuse* (Boulogne, 1935).

4. For the eleven properties of the sphere, see David Hilbert and Stephan Cohn-Vossen, *Geometry and the Imagination* (New York, 1952), pp. 215–32.

5. For a full discussion of the arrow as a diagrammatic symbol, see Paul Klee, *Pedagogical Sketchbook* (New York, 1953), pp. 54-57.

6. See any elementary textbook on organic chemistry. Also, for a graphic presentation, see Max Bill, *Form* (Basel, 1952), p. 19.

7. Theo van Doesburg, *Grundbegriffe der neuen gestaltenden Kunst,* Bauhausbücher No. 6 (Munich, 1924), illustrations 3, 4, 11, 31. Though van Doesburg did not intend his drawings in this way, but only as an exploration of formal possibilities, it can hardly be a coincidence that these drawings coincide, in time, with the birth of an architecture based on rectilinear components.

8. For actual bridges which have this diagrammatic quality very strongly, see Maillart's bridges in Max Bill, *Maillart* (Zurich, 1955), esp. p. 40. The engineer Nervi also has a good deal to say about the use of diagrams; see Pier Luigi Nervi, *Structures* (New York, 1956), pp. 17–26, 97.

9. Of course, the required street widths will not be in exact proportion to the flow densities; flow viscosity, parked cars, etc., mean that the number of vehicles per hour in a given direction is not related linearly to the width required to accommodate them. But the basic organization of the new form will still be that given by the pattern of the diagram.

10. The problem of soap films was first solved by Joseph Plateau, *Statique expérimentale et théorique des liquides soumis aux seules forces moléculaires* (Paris, 1873). For recent discussions see D'Arcy Wentworth Thompson, *On Growth and Form*, 2nd ed. (Cambridge, 1959), pp. 365–77; and a beautiful little book by C. V. Boys, *Soap Bubbles and the Forces Which Mold Them*, Doubleday Anchor Science Study Series (New York, 1959).

11. This does not mean, in any sense, that function is capable of defining form; for any one functional program there will usually be many possible forms.

12. François de Pierrefeu and Le Corbusier, *La Maison des hommes* (Paris, 1942).

13. *Encyclopaedia Britannica*, 14th edition, article on "Aeronautics."

14. Robert W. Marks, *The Dymaxion World of Buckminster Fuller* (New York, 1960).

15. Many "projects," which remain unbuilt, but indicate certain extreme possibilities, are really "hypotheses" about particular aspects of some problem. See, for instance, the projects exhibited in 1960 at the Museum of Modern Art under the title "Visionary Architecture," described in Arthur Drexler, "Visionary Architecture," *Arts and Architecture*, 78:10–13 (January 1961).

16. The vital part played by lucid notation in the invention of new mathematics is a striking instance of this. See Ludwig Wittgenstein, *Remarks on the Foundations of Mathematics* (Oxford, 1956), pp. 47, 73, 78, 82.

17. See Appendix 1, pp. 154–173.

Chapter Eight: Definitions

1. In some cases where a designer has explicitly broken his intentions down into a specific list of requirements the list he produces has almost exactly the character of a set of misfit variables. See, for example, A. and P. Smithson, "Criteria for Mass Housing," in Oscar Newman, ed., *New Frontiers in Architecture: CIAM '59 in Otterlo* (New York, 1961), p. 79.

2. In the text which follows, we shall speak interchangeably of meeting the requirement x, of avoiding the misfit x, and of the variable x taking the value 0; and similarly of failing to meet the requirement x, of the misfit x occurring, and of the variable x taking the value 1.

3. Naturally enough, there is always a time lag between the introduction of some new scale and the time when its value can be established predictively for any given form. Thus the sabin, a measure of acoustic

absorption, was introduced in the 1920's. Even now, 1963, the absorption of an auditorium of complicated shape can still not be predicted, and needs to be determined experimentally. See Wallace C. Sabine, *Collected Papers* (Cambridge, Mass., 1922); V. O. Knudsen, *Architectural Acoustics* (New York, 1932), pp. 119–239.

4. See any typical handbook. For instance, the Dodge Corporation's *Time-Saver Standards: A Manual of Essential Architectural Data* (New York, 1946).

5. Herbert Simon has introduced the concept of "satisficing," as a more accurate picture than "optimization" of what we actually do in complex decision situations. See his three papers, "Rationality and Administrative Decision Making," "A Behavioral Model of Rational Choice," and "Rational Choice and the Structure of the Environment," all published in *Models of Man* (New York, 1957), esp. pp. 204–5, 247–52, and 261–71. Also see James G. March and Herbert A. Simon, *Organizations* (New York, 1958), pp. 140–41.

6. *Ibid.*, pp. 162–63.

7. Karl R. Popper, *The Open Society and Its Enemies* (Princeton, 1950), p. 155. "The piecemeal engineer will, accordingly, adopt the method of searching for, and fighting against, the greatest and most urgent evils of society, rather than searching for, and fighting for, its greatest ultimate good." Also called "social engineering" by Roscoe Pound, *Introduction to the Philosophy of Law* (New Haven, 1922), p. 99. For an economic example see C. G. F. Simkin, "Budgetary Reform," *Economic Record*, 17 (1941):192ff, and 18 (1942):16ff.

8. To convince ourselves that this domain D is in principle finite (though of course very large), we must first put arbitrary limits on the actual physical size of the form to be designed. It doesn't matter what size we choose, we can make these limits wide enough to cover anything imaginable. In the case of a drinking-water heater, which must go inside a house, it isn't unreasonable for instance, to expect that even taking its possibly very complex relation with other fitments in the house into consideration, it should not occupy a space larger than 10 meters by 10 meters by 10 meters. Suppose we consider a cubical volume, 10 meters on an edge. It isn't unreasonable to assume that any kettle will fit into it. Divide the cube, by means of a three-dimensional grid, into small cubical cells. Let us say, for the sake of argument, that we choose cells which are 1 micron (1/1000 mm) on an edge. There are then $(10^7)^3$ or 10^{21} of these in the cube. Now let us consider the possibility of filling each one of these cells, independently, cell by cell, with one of 1,000,000 materials (including air, copper, water, silica, etc.). There are then $(10^6)^{10^{21}}$, or roughly $10^{10^{27}}$, different possible ways of arranging our materials, distributing our materials among the cells. (Writing three zeros per second, it would

take 10^{12} centuries to write this number down in full.) Let us call each one of these ways a possible configuration. And let us call the set of all $10^{10^{22}}$ possible configurations, the domain D of possible configurations. *Most* of the configurations, like the distribution of air and water in alternating cells, are clearly absurd. But it is also evident that any conceivable kind of kettle corresponds to one of the $10^{10^{22}}$ configurations in the domain D. For the discussion of such domains (what statisticians often call "sample spaces") see William Feller, *An Introduction to Probability Theory and Its Applications*, I (New York, 1957), 7–25.

9. *Ibid.*, I, 114.

10. G. U. Yule and M. G. Kendall, *An Introduction to the Theory of Statistics*, 14th ed. (London, 1950), pp. 19–29. We can also compare $p(x_i = 1)$ with $p(x_i = 1/x_j = 0)$ — the probability of x_i occurring given that x_j does *not* occur. Or $p(x_i = 0)$ with $p(x_i = 0/x_j = 1)$. There are eight such tests. While they are the same in the case of independence, in the case of dependence they are four slightly different cases, and it is therefore more usual to estimate the common difference which is symmetrical; cf. p. 29.

11. Yule and Kendall, p. 271. This function (the product moment correlation coefficient is also equal to χ^2/N; *ibid.*, p. 272.

12. Requirements are *not* connected simply because they seem in some sense similar. In particular, for instance, the kind of connection we see on account of the fact that two variables have both "to do with acoustics" has no physical implications, and is therefore irrelevant. Here again the language would have become unjustifiably compulsive; for it is to some large extent accidental that we have a concept called "acoustics."

We must be careful too, not to think requirements connected because of what seem like good design ideas. It seems sensible perhaps, to give a house a service core containing kitchen, laundry, plumbing, bathrooms. But the fact that the service core simultaneously meets several requirements does not, per se, make these requirements connected.

13. See p. 109.

14. R. B. Braithwaite, *Scientific Explanation* (Cambridge, 1953), pp. 257–64, 367–68.

15. This is rather like the idea of interpreting the probability of an event as a property of the situation governing that event, rather than the limiting frequency of its occurrence over a number of trials. See Karl R. Popper, "The Propensity Interpretation of the Calculus of Probability, and the Quantum Theory," in *Observation and Interpretation*, ed. by S. Körner, Proceedings of the Ninth Symposium of the Colston Research Society, Bristol (London, 1957), pp. 65–70, and the comment by D. Bohm on page 82 of the same volume. See also W. Kneale *Probability and Induction* (Oxford, 1949), p. 198.

16. For the isomorphism between dyadic relations and graphs see Denes König, *Theorie der endlichen und unendlichen Graphen* (New York, 1950), pp. 107–9, and Claude Berge, *Théorie des graphes et ses applications* (Paris, 1958), p. 6. Also for the isomorphism of dyadic relations and square matrices see Irving M. Copilowish, "Matrix Developments of the Calculus of Relations," *Journal of Symbolic Logic*, 13:193–203 (December 1948). For the extensional definition of a relation as the set of pairs related under it, see Alfred Tarski, "On the Calculus of Relations," *Journal of Symbolic Logic*, 6:73–89 (March 1941).

17. In fact, as we shall see in Appendix 2, p. 187, the distinction between positive and negative links is irrelevant, and we only need to establish L, not L^+ and L^- separately. We shall also find it convenient in practice to put $v = 1$, so that v_{ij} can only be 0 or 1.

18. It is sometimes quite hard to draw the graph in a simple way, so that the links are not all tangled. For a way to draw graphs, given the matrix of links, see a recent paper published in the *Journal of the Acoustical Society of America*, 33 (1961):1183, on "Realization of a Linear Graph Given Its Algebraic Specification."

19. See Appendix 2, p. 177.

20. See Appendix 2, p. 177.

21. See Appendix 2, p. 175.

22. Let us note that this condition of equal "size" only refers to the purely formal character of the system of variables. It does not imply that the different variables have equal importance in the solution of the problem. If it is more important to meet one requirement than another, this still has no place in an analysis of the problem's causal structure, but must be handled as it arises during the realization of the program.

23. We know that we shall never find requirements which are *totally* independent. If we could, we could satisfy them one after the other, without ever running into conflicts. The very problem of design springs from the fact that this is not possible because of the field character of the form-context interaction.

24. See the list of variables given in the worked example, Appendix 1, pp. 137–142.

Chapter Nine: Solution

1. For a general discussion see Max Wertheimer, "Untersuchungen zur Lehre von Gestalt, II," *Psychologische Forschung*, 4 (1923):301–50, translated in shortened form in *Readings in Perception*, ed. by David C. Beardslee and Michael Wertheimer (New York, 1958), pp. 115–35, for a specific reference to this point, see Wolfgang Kohler, *Gestalt Psychology* (New York, 1929), pp. 148–86.

2. L. S. Pontryagin, *Foundations of Combinatorial Topology* (New York, 1952), p. 13. The practical aspects of this method have been developed chiefly by writers on sociometry: Frank Harary and Ian C. Ross, "A Procedure for Clique Detection Using the Group Matrix," *Sociometry*, 20:205-15 (September 1957); R. Duncan Luce and A. D. Perry, "A Method of Matrix Analysis of Group Structure," *Psychometrika*, 14 (1949):95-116; R. D. Luce, "Connectivity and Generalized Cliques in Sociometric Group Structure," *Psychometrika*, 15 (1950):169-90; Denes König, *Theorie der endlichen und undendlichen Graphen* (New York, 1950), pp. 224-37; Claude Berge, *Théorie des graphes et ses applications* (Paris, 1958), pp. 195, 201; G. A. Dirac, "Some Theorems on Abstract Graphs," *Proceedings of the London Mathematical Society*, 3.2 (1952), 69. See also W. Ross Ashby, *Design for a Brain* (New York, 1960), p. 169; R. Duncan Luce, "Two Decomposition Theorems for a Class of Finite Oriented Graphs," *American Journal of Mathematics*, 74:701-22, esp. 703 (July 1952); H. Whitney, "Non-separable and Planar Graphs," *Transactions of the American Mathematical Society*, 34 (1932):339-62, and "Congruent Graphs and the Connectivity of Graphs," *American Journal of* Mathematics, 54 (1932):150; A. Shimbel, "Structural Parameters of Communications Networks," *Bulletin of Mathematical Biophysics*, 15 (1953):501-7, and "Structure in Communication Nets," *Proceedings of the Symposium on Information Networks*, April 1954, Polytechnic Institute, Brooklyn (1955); Satosi Watanabe, "Concept Formation and Classification by Information — Theoretical Correlation Analysis," letter to the editor, *IBM Journal of Research and Development*, January 30, 1961.

Perhaps the broadest discussion is to be found in Kurt Lewin, *Field Theory in Social Science* (New York, 1951), in the appendix called "Analysis of the Concepts Whole, Differentiation, and Unity," pp. 305-38, esp. pp. 305-11.

3. Luce, "Two Decomposition Theorems," p. 703.

4. In practice *G* will usually be connected; that is, there is a path of links connecting every two vertices. It is then, of course, impossible to find a partition which cuts no links, and we are reduced to finding one across which there is the least, rather than no, interaction. It is worth pointing out right away that it is only possible to look for such minimum interaction partitions because the interactions are probabilistic. As Ashby has pointed out, in a connected system with deterministic linkages, even when every variable is not immediately linked to every other, the system behaves as if it were, so that no one part is less connected to the rest than any other, and it means nothing to compare degrees of independence. Ross Ashby, *Design for a Brain*, 1st. ed. (London, 1952), pp. 161-62, 251-52.

5. See Appendix 2, pp. 176-184.

6. See Appendix 2, p. 190.

7. Ludwig von Bertalanffy, *Problems of Life* (New York, 1960), pp. 37–47.

8. The following note must be appended to this conjecture. If it is true that the causal structure of the problem actually defines the physical constituents of a successful form, we naturally wish to know whether the result of the analysis is independent of the particular set of variables which have been chosen to describe the problem. It is clear that the same problem might have been stated in terms of an altogether different set of variables, which as a whole covers the same ground, but breaks it up differently. This new set would then be clustered in different sets and systems. But would the content of these new systems, or to put it more concretely, the physical components they implied, have been the same. Intuition suggests strongly that this would be so. Indeed, I feel that some sort of invariance theorem of this sort is necessary as a secure foundation for the whole method (like showing that the properties of a vector space are invariant for different bases); but I have not yet succeeded in finding a proof of such a theorem.

Appendix Two: Mathematical Treatment of Decomposition

1. See the previous references to graph theory given in Chapter 6, note 11.

2. G. U. Yule and M. G. Kendall, *An Introduction to the Theory of Statistics*, 14th ed. (London, 1950), p. 272.

3. *Ibid.*, pp. 35, 281.

4. *Ibid.*, pp. 35–36.

5. William Feller, *An Introduction to Probability Theory and Its Applications*, I (New York, 1957), p. 22.

6. *Ibid.*, p. 22.

7. *Ibid.*

8. Because we have artificially made $p(x_i = 0) = \frac{1}{2}$, this probability distribution must not be confused with the proportions of misfits in the domain of solutions D. In that case, $p(x_i = 0)$ is small compared with $p(x_i = 1)$. The present distribution is designed solely to give us the decomposition of the system: it only reflects the actual behavior of the variables as far as their correlations are concerned.

9. See Chapter 8, p. 112.

10. C. E. Shannon and W. Weaver, *The Mathematical Theory of Communication* (Urbana, Ill., 1949), pp. 18–22.

11. See note 17 to Chapter 8.

12. Satosi Watanabe, "Information Theoretical Analysis of Multi-

variate Correlation," *IBM Journal of Research and Development*, 4:69 (January 1960).

13. See note 17 to Chapter 8.

14. Feller, *Probability Theory*, p. 213.

15. To normalize a random variable X, we replace it by $(X-\mu)/\sigma$, where μ is the mean and σ^2 the variance. See Feller, p. 215.

16. We remember that $l_0 = \frac{1}{2}m(m-1)$, $l^\pi = \sum_\pi v_{ij}$, $l_0^\pi = \sum_\pi s_\alpha s_\beta$.

17. Christopher Alexander and Marvin Manheim, *HIDECS 2: A Computer Program for the Hierarchical Decomposition of a Set with an Associated Graph*, M.I.T. Civil Engineering Systems Laboratory Publication No. 160 (Cambridge, Mass., 1962); and Christopher Alexander, *HIDECS 3: Four Computer Programs for the Hierarchical Decomposition of Systems Which Have an Associated Linear Graph*, M.I.T. Civil Engineering Systems Laboratory Research Report R63-27 (Cambridge, Mass., 1963).